Feltmaking

*F*eltmaking

Deborah McGavock
and Christine Lewis

The Art of Crafts

First published in 2000 by
The Crowood Press Ltd
Ramsbury, Marlborough
Wiltshire SN8 2HR

British Library Cataloguing-in-Publication Data
A catalogue record for this book is available from the British Library.

ISBN 1 86126 308 2

Acknowledgements
With thanks to Judy Scarland who taught us to make felt all those years ago. Also to our
husbands, John and Richard, for their help and cleverness with computers, and to
Deborah's mother, Adelaide, for her encouragement.

Thanks to Jenny Cowern, Jeanette Appleton, Rutsuko Sataka and Janet Ledsham for
supplying photographs. Other photographs by Jacky Phillips, unless credited separately.

Line drawings by Graham Kent.

Photograph previous page: Jenny Cowern, 'Sandstone Rock and Tide 3', hand-made felt,
colours blended skilfully to achieve a water-colour effect.

Typeface used: Melior © Adobe Systems Inc.

Designed and typeset by Annette Findlay
Printed and bound by Leo Paper Products, China

Contents

Preface

Feltmaking is addictive: once you've tried it, you get hooked. It is also a very seductive medium, seeming to have a life of its own, yet easy to tame. We hope this book will inspire you to make felt: clear, step-by-step instructions are given in a series of projects which will take you from the beginners' workshop to masterclass. En route you'll learn something about sheep and wool, the historical and anthropological background to feltmaking, and its mythology. We'll introduce you to artists and craftspeople who are taking feltmaking to the outer limits today, and you'll discover the feltmaking of people who lived two thousand years ago or more.

The raw materials and equipment for feltmaking are inexpensive and easily acquired. Studio space can be the kitchen table, and from there you are limited only by your imagination, time and energy. Felting can be like painting with wool, or a way of making a functional object, or a bit of both. The result can be any shape, two-dimensional or three-dimensional as you wish. The fashion-aware can create a hat, a jacket or footwear; the sculptor a vessel or jewellery; the toy-maker a puppet or even a bouncy ball.

WHAT IS FELT?

Felt is a textile, a non-woven fabric. It consists of tangled wool fibres which, after they have been soaked and pounded, have matted together in all directions to form a dense fabric. The unique structure of the wool fibre makes this possible. It is made of a series of scales, which overlap from the root of the sheep's wool fibre up to the tip. When you pour hot water onto the wool fibres, the scales open up. Then when you rub it, roll it, pound it or tread it, the scales interlock and close up tighter than ever.

UNEXPECTED PLACES TO FIND FELT

Felt does not fray when it is cut, so it does not need to be hemmed; this is one of its chief advantages, and makes it an excellent textile for use in many industries. If you look around, you'll find felt in lots of unexpected places. Until very recently the BCW Felting Factory, established in the 1780s, made felt in England for use in pianos, for instance for customers such as Yamaha; it also made felt for diamond polishers and cabinet makers' wood polishers. The green baize on pool tables and card tables is felt, and the fashion business has used felt in the shoulder pads, collars and lapels of coats and jackets, and for shoe insoles. In the house you might find felt underlay for the carpet, felt buttons on the mattress, felt upholstery linings in your chairs, and felt carpet tiles; and if you happen to have a 1940s or 1950s teapot with a built-in metal cosy, have a look inside at the felt linings. In the car you might find felt in the filters, gaskets, soundproofing and carpets.

The overlapping scale structure of wool fibre.

Opposite: Janet Ledsham, 'Canopy', based on kepenek and traditional hooded cloak worn in Ireland until the eighteenth century.

1 The Origins of Feltmaking

MYTHOLOGY

Every craft has its own mythology, and felt is no exception. Many of the stories probably hold a grain of truth, and each demonstrates the simplicity of the technique. One of our favourites concerns the pair of sheep in Noah's Ark: the hold of the Ark must have been warm and cramped, and the sheep would have shed their wool onto the floor, and trampled it and urinated onto it – and once all the animals had left the Ark, Noah found a felt rug! Mount Ararat, the landing place of the Ark, is in Eastern Turkey where felt may genuinely have originated.

Perhaps Joseph's coat of many colours, made by his father, Jacob, was made of felt. Certainly we know of felt coats or mantles still worn by shepherds today in Turkey.

In early Christian times, St Clement (the patron saint of hatters) and St Christopher (the patron saint of travellers) were each on the run at different times. It is said that the fleeing saints took off their sandals and wrapped their sore feet in scraps of fleece plucked from the hedges, then replaced their sandals and continued on their hot and sweaty way; at the journey's end, the wool had turned into a felt sock. This proves that all you need to make felt is a fleece, warm water and a measure of agitation.

Felt had many magical and religious associations for ancient nomadic peoples. The Mongols made felt idols which they believed guarded their sheep, watched over their families and took care of their ancestors. When a tomb at Pazyryk was opened, four fabulous stuffed white felt swans were found perched on the corners of a covered wooden wagon: it is thought that these were considered to have symbolic powers, and were there to transport the souls of the dead.

In many tribes white felt is still highly regarded, and is thought to bring good luck. Animals would be sacrificed on it, and in a marriage ceremony the bride sits on a white felt rug, as do some newly elected tribal chieftains. In Mary Burkett's book *The Art of the Feltmaker* there is an account taken from the Pei Shih annals of the Northern Dynasties AD 529 which describes how the Emperor was lifted on black felt to symbolize his obeisance to Heaven. The same black felt covered the

Stuffed felt swan found at Pazyryk.

Opposite: Rutsuko Sakata, garments in wool, silk and gauze.

seven dignitaries who were lifting him, thus symbolizing their obeisance to the Emperor.

THE FACTS

We do know that felt is the oldest textile fabric. People learnt to make felt before they could spin, weave or knit, probably during the Bronze Age. It is quite possible that sheep were the first animals to be domesticated after dogs, providing milk and meat and, as a by-product, their skins for clothing. The ancient nomadic shepherds could well have made their beds more comfortable with a padding of plucked wool, and after a few nights' sleep, found felt which they eventually adapted for wearing in place of skins.

The traditional shepherd's cloak still worn today in Turkey is called a *kepenek*. It is a very simple garment without sleeves, with an opening at the front, in the middle; it is undyed, with only a black maker's mark, and can weigh anything up to 6kg. It protects the shepherd from cold, heat, dust and rain. At Housestead Fort, on Hadrian's Wall in Northumberland, what appear to be similar garments can be seen on carved stone figures. There is also another figure, in a relief carving, of a Roman soldier in a felt tunic, and historian Mary Burkett has a theory that his helmet would actually have been a pointed felt cap such as those worn by the Phrygians.

Although there appears to be little written evidence regarding the origins of felt, there are references from many sources to help us build up a picture. The earliest archaeological evidence, albeit not of actual felt, dates from 6500–6300BC and was found in a Neolithic excavation at Catal Huyuk in present-day Turkey: here there is a wall-painting of 'whirling curvilinear motifs' drawn in a beige colour and outlined in black on a white

ground. In her book, Mary Burkett argues that these patterns and edgings are very similar to the felt appliqué techniques still practised in Kyrgyzstan and Mongolia today.

In the fourth century BC the Chinese called the nomads' territory the 'land of felt'. From their writing we know that warriors had felt shields and hats, and gradually the nomads' felt became more commonly used in Chinese households and for clothing.

Felt was used extensively by the military up to, and even during, the twentieth century. Between the fifteenth and eighteenth centuries the Osman sultans in Turkey equipped their armies for over 300 years with felt clothing, including headwear with shoulder-length white felt neck protectors, also boots and saddle blankets, thereby giving employment to hundreds of feltmakers in Constantinople alone; it was only in the 1950s that the Turkish military stopped wearing felt boots. The Cossack armies were known as the 'felt troops' because of the amount of felt worn by the soldiers: in a thick layer it protected them from enemy weapons, as well as from the wind and rain. Roman soldiers toughened their felt armour and boots by pickling them in vinegar.

Tight-fitting felt caps were *de rigueur* at the theatre, and freed slaves were proud to wear a felt cap called a *pileus* (from the Greek word *pilos*, meaning 'felt') as a sign of their status. If you travel to Pompeii you can see what is probably the oldest surviving illustration of feltmaking depicted on a wall-painting. Recently, while browsing in an antique shop in Scotland, Mary Burkett found a drawing illustrating the use of felt to line a metal breastplate and helmet. Felt is the perfect material for linings as it is soft and pliable, and would protect the skin from rubbing against the metal.

Some of the oldest felts still in existence were found in a surprising discov-

The Phrygian cap.

ery in China, in the Xinjang region. There are three burial sites at Hami, Loulan and Chechen between the Talimak desert and the Tian Sian mountains: the oldest contains the 4,000-year-old mummy of a tall woman known as the Beauty of Loulan, and she wears a felt bonnet with a feather in it; there is also a 2m (6ft 6in) Chechen man who wears long, red-and-green-patterned felt puttees. This particular find was not widely reported in the West, but there was a touring exhibition in Japan and the catalogue was sent to Mary Burkett by Jori Johnson, an American felt-maker who lives and works there. The exhibition was called 'The Kingdom of Loulan – Eternal Beauty' and from the catalogue it is possible to identify five items of felt which pre-date the finds from Pazyryk, which until then were the earliest known: there is a woman's black pointed felt hat (perhaps indicating that she had two husbands), a shoe made of animal skins and lined with felt, and a white felt sock, all dating from the ninth century BC.

The Pazyryk finds in the frozen tombs of the Altai Mountains in Siberia, Asia, excavated between 1929 and 1949 by Sergei Rudenko, have proved the most significant of all. They include objects and felts dating from 600—200BC, beautifully preserved by the area's permafrost, and because the material has been kept in such good condition, today we have a clear idea of the way of life of this ancient nomadic people. There were 212 tumuli, or burial chambers, built with timber in large deep holes, their walls covered with felt wall-hangings. The dead person's possessions were packed in on top of their body: clothes, including felt socks and stockings; cushions, rugs and carpets; women's hair decorations in felt; saddle covers, blankets, even horses and wagons. Their blankets and tents had felt decorations, and the wide variety of felts found in the tombs shows just how important

this material was in their everyday life – and the fact that it was used decoratively shows that the Altai people considered it to be an art as well as a craft: they had time for the beauty of things.

Although these nomadic people had no written language, they composed wonderful scenes of animals, birds and mythological creatures such as griffins and dragons. As artists they were confident in their use of materials, and freely mixed felt with woven cloth, fur, leather, horsehair, sinews and metal, as well as wood, bones, feathers and shells. Sometimes holes were cut out to reveal a different coloured layer of felt underneath, or leather and thread wrapped with a fine metal would be used to couch the seams. Their sheep provided the raw material for felt, and this material they traded east as far as China, and west towards Turkey and Hungary. These stunning felts are now in the Pazyryk room of the Hermitage Museum, St Petersburg.

Similar finds were discovered at Noin-Ula in the northern Mongolian mountains, including some large felt carpets decorated with appliqué dating from the first century AD.

In the Far East, countries such as China, Japan and Korea are more usually associated with silk, as sheep farming in these regions is a relatively recent occupation. But wool is likely to have been imported along the Silk Road, and some beautiful felts have been discovered; moreover the ancient Japanese emperors built vast depots within their palaces to house their treasures – the last one known to have been built, in AD756 at Shoso-In, has inlaid patterned felt rugs in classic Tang style using pale yellow, green, blue and red on a white background. These can be seen once a year in exhibitions arranged by the National Museum in Nara, the ancient capital city of Japan. Many more are in private collections in Kyoto but have been seen by Jori Johnson.

Pointed felt hat.

In *Echoes*, the journal of the International Feltmakers Association, she describes felt mats beautifully decorated with scrolls, flowers and borders; these were probably intended to be boards for the game 'Go'. Feltmaking now thrives in Japan and Korea.

THE ROOTS OF CONTEMPORARY FELTMAKING

Today feltmaking takes place in practically every country in the world: wherever there are sheep, there is the potential to make felt. The southern hemisphere, famous for wool production in New Zealand, Australia and the Falklands, exports good quality fleeces all over the world, and the feltmakers also travel, teaching their skills and learning from other people. The same is happening in North America and Canada, where news of new techniques and equipment travels faster than ever thanks to the internet.

In Scandinavia and northern Europe there are feltmaking traditions in socks, footwear, headwear and toymaking, and today these skills are taught, experimented with and modernized by a huge number of artists whose wonderful felts can be seen in exhibitions and on web-

The cradle of feltmaking.

sites. Great British and Danish explorers have filled museums with large collections of ethnological felts, which anyone can draw, photograph and learn from.

Hungarian feltmakers carry on the toy-making tradition, and some of their work is displayed at the toy museum at Kecskemet, set up by Istvan Vidak and Mari Nagy: these two feltmakers – who are also inspirational teachers – hold courses and organize exhibitions. Mehmet Girgic is another famous feltmaker; he frequently travels to England to demonstrate at the prestigious 'Art in Action' event near Oxford. He has over thirty years' experience of feltmaking, having learnt the skills from his father and grandfather; he makes rugs, *kepeneks* and Whirling Dervishes' *sikke* hats in his workshop in Konya, Turkey.

The cradle of feltmaking, the source of worldwide skills today, must surely be in Central Asia. Traditional felt, made as it has been for hundreds of years, is still used in the everyday lives of the men and women of Turkmenistan, Uzbekistan, Kyrgyzstan, Kazakhstan and parts of Mongolia and China. These nomadic people still make their tent-like homes, known as yurts, out of felt. Their bags, rugs and clothing are also of hand-made felt; these are replaced every year as they wear out.

There have been yurts in Central Asia for almost 2,000 years. Small clay models and toys dating from 950BC have been excavated around Azerbaijan, and others from 460BC were discovered in the frozen tombs of Pazyryk. In 460BC Herodotus wrote of Scythians living in felt tents on carts and in white felt tents around trees. However, there are very few remains of these tents since it was the custom of some nomads to burn all the belongings pertaining to a dead person, and this included their tents.

The following eighth-century poem by Po Chu-i is the first verbal description of a Central Asian yurt:

Yurt. (Photo Stephanie Bunn)

The Blue Felt Tent

The fine fleece from a thousand sheep is
    brought together
Hundreds of arcs are fitted together tautly
The round skeleton and the willow
    staves of the sides are strong
It is dyed fresh in the dark blue of the
    northern sky
Made in the north, assembled by
    tribesmen
It came south in the train of Barbarian
    prisoners
Even the strongest wind is unable to
    move it
And it is most tautly resistant to the rain
It has a roof rising to a point in the middle
It has no corners and is round in the
    four directions
Soft and warm, felt rolls are laid about
And twanging bundles of pipes and
    strings
It is especially suitable when the ground
    is covered in frost
It might well be called sky amidst the
    snow

(Whaley 1949)

The tent itself is called a *ger*, which means 'a small world within a big world'; strictly speaking, the term 'yurt' refers to the site on which a *ger* is erected. It is made of a circular, collapsible wooden frame covered with several layers of felt in bands which wrap around the base and cover the roof. The outer bands are usually decorated with symbols, or tell a folk story. The roof is made of four pieces of felt sewn together like a skirt and pulled tightly with cord at the crown to give a neat fit.

Inside the tent, richly decorated carpets cover the entire floor. They are used to sit and to sleep on; piled high, they are a sign of wealth. The shape of the dome varies between tribes, as does the style of the doorway; for example, a Kyrghyz yurt usually has a felt flap, whereas the Mongolian yurt has a wooden door, sometimes covered with felt.

In these communities, feltmaking is usually a group activity at the end of the summer, when the sheep have been sheared. Often it is a festive occasion, with people working together in large

Yurt with decorated door
flap. (Photo Stephanie Bunn)

groups. The women prepare the fleece by washing it, and when it has dried, they beat it with willow sticks to separate and fluff up the fibres. After dying, nowadays with synthetic dyes, it is laid out on a reed mat called a *chij* until the layers are about 30cm (12in) deep. A little hot water and soap is sprinkled on top, then the whole lot is rolled up in the *chij* ready for the rolling and kicking to take place. This is hard, physical work, and each community has its own favourite way of doing it: in Mongolia, for instance, the new felt is made on top of an old felt instead of the *chij*; this old felt is known as the 'Mother of Felt', and after being rolled up it is dragged behind horses across the steppes for about three hours. The resultant new felt is called the 'Daughter Felt'.

Each area has its own striking and distinctive patterns and colours, handed down through generations of women. In Kyrghizstan and Kazakhstan they make wonderful 'shyrdak' or mosaic felts. The master, always a woman, draws the pattern freehand on top of two layers of contrasting colour felts, which are then cut and reassembled to form a perfect mirror image. Many fine examples of Kyrghiz felts, as well as *kepeneks* from Iran and Turkey, can be viewed by appointment at the Museum of Mankind, and at the Horniman Museum in London.

Although the Turkmen of Turkmenistan are more famous for their carpet-making, they also make felt of a very high quality, rich in colour and with unique designs for household and prayer rugs.

HATS IN ANCIENT AND CONTEMPORARY FELTMAKING

Hatmaking is a tradition in many countries, and one which has played an important part in many cultures through the ages. Hats featured in the

Women laying out the pattern on to a *chij*. (Photo Stephanie Bunn)

Pazyryk and Xinjang finds, indicating that headwear was often worn for ceremonies, or that it signified marital status: a newly-married woman would wear a tall hat until after the birth of her first child, when she would pass it on to the nubile daughter. Images of caps or hats can be seen in ancient sculptures and relief carvings in Persepolis and Housesteads. During the French Revolution the Jacobeans wore a battered version of the Phrygian cap, which they saw as a symbol of freedom.

In South America, the Spanish introduced feltmaking to Ecuador. Some indigenous groups there have managed to keep their cultural identity, including textile traditions, through both the Inca and Spanish conquests. Felt hats are part of the national dress worn every day by the men and women of Ecuador, and they are still made by family groups living in Ilmen, near Otalavo. They use brightly coloured, pre-felted wool for their hats and horse blankets.

It was not only the militia of the Ottoman Empire that wore felt hats: it was also compulsory for civilians, who had to wear a fez – a small, pillbox felt hat dyed either red or black, with a tassel; even women had to wear it under the veil.

The Whirling Dervishes, a religious sect founded in the thirteenth century, wore a tall felt hat, or *sikke*, until they were prohibited from dancing by Kemal Ataturk in 1924. Since the 1950s their culture has been revived, although the art of making the *sikke* had almost been forgotten – fortunately feltmaker Mehmet Girgic had learnt the skill from his grandfather, and after some experimentation has been able to revive it.

On display in the Royal Cornwall Museum in Truro, Cornwall, is a miner's felt hat which had been bought in Redruth in 1930. It is only about 3mm (⅛in) thick, but very stiff, probably hardened with resin and urine. A similar miner's helmet made in Bradwell, Derbyshire, is on display in Skipton Museum, and another miner's hat can be seen in the Manx Museum on the Isle of Man. In this museum's 1906 catalogue there are references to equipment for the preparation of wool to make 'Beaver' hats, an industry which had died out in the Isle of Man before 1881.

Throughout the UK, Europe and Scandinavia there are hat museums testifying to once-thriving hatmaking industries. And, of course, felt hats are still made in Luton today.

2 Equipment and Materials

You may already have much of the equipment necessary to make felt, or the items you need may be easily and cheaply bought in charity shops or at car-boot sales. These should include the following:

Old towels: These will be a good base to work on, and are needed to soak up excess soapy water.

Old polyester or nylon net curtains: Use a fairly open design. Bear in mind that you will need a piece of net approximately double the size of the felt that you want to make.

A rush beachmat or an old wooden slatted window blind (if you can find a cheap one) with the fittings removed. This is used in the rolling method and is a good source of friction.

Old detergent bottles or **old plastic containers** with a hole punched in each lid. Or use a **plant or laundry spray mister**.

A broom handle or a **wooden rolling pin**. This is needed to give a rigid centre when rolling the fibres in a rush beachmat.

Plastic bags or **polystyrene pizza bases**. These will be used for resist techniques when making hats and glove puppets. **Bubble-wrap** can also be used for resist techniques.

Wool carders: These are used for preparing fleece, or for blending fibres and colours. Hand-held carders are adequate for small quantities, but if you want to prepare whole fleeces you will need a drum carder.

Hat blocks or an **upturned basin** on which to shape your hat.

Shoe last, or **the foot** of the intended wearer of slippers and shoes.

Wool fleece: Before you acquire this vital commodity, *see* the section 'Understanding Wool', below, p. 20.

Some equipment needed for feltmaking.

Drum carder, hand carder and hat block.

YOUR FELTING WORKPLACE

The great joy of feltmaking is its accessibility, the fact that it needs no special studio or equipment. We like to make felt in the kitchen where hot water is to hand, and where there are surfaces at the right height, and large enough on which to work. The draining board by the sink is ideal as it provides some friction, and excess water can drain away. However, it is important to consider the height of your work surface carefully as you will be standing at it and working on it for some time. If, after about 30 minutes, you feel discomfort in your lower back, or that you are bending down too much, you should move to a new work surface or alter the height of the table. Blocks of wood could

be placed under the legs to raise the height: ideally the surface should be just below the height of your elbows. When you start working again there should be a noticeable difference.

Don't work for too long at a stretch – so once you have reached a particular goal in the work, take a break. Make a point of shifting your leg position from time to time to redistribute your weight, and when using the rolling technique, try to keep your arms and wrists straight so that you use the whole length of your arms from fingertips to elbows. It's also good exercise for your tummy muscles when you use the natural weight of your body and a forwards-and-backwards rocking motion.

As a beginner you are likely to make quite small pieces at first; then as your knowledge and understanding of the

Opposite: Christine Lewis, 'Salamander', felt, printed and machine embroidered.

To get the most satisfaction from your first feltmaking experience, it is best not to use the fleece from your neighbour's pet sheep. As you become more confident you should experiment with blending different sheep fibres together, or using different fibres for special effects, such as the beautiful curl of Wensleydale. You could also try blending other animal hairs with wool: combine dog or cat hair, Angora rabbit, camel, llama, alpaca, goat – even human hair. Some plant fibres can be blended with wool to make felt. Silk works well, and the finished felt has a beautiful sheen. Look at the photographs of Deborah Roberts' laminated Nuno felt with silk to see what is possible.

process develops, you may want to make a larger piece. This is where your large beachmat or wooden slatted window blind can have a dual purpose: lay the blind or mat onto the floor, place the net on top, then the fibres. When your design is complete, cover with net, roll up the blind and carry to a suitable work surface to be rolled. Alternatively, in good weather, and given some willing helpers, large pieces of felt can be foot-rolled outside!

Sometimes you may want to complete a large feltwork in the washing machine. As no two washing machines are the same you really need to make some experiments to get the best results. Before putting the felt in the machine, stitch it securely on each side inside the netting so that it does not felt into a ball.

UNDERSTANDING WOOL

Most animal fibres are suitable for felt-making, but wool is best. For the new-comer to feltmaking, the best wool to use is undoubtedly merino, from Australia's main breed of sheep. It has good shrink-age, and can be relied upon to felt quickly. As you become more experi-enced in feltmaking, your knowledge of wool and sheep will also grow: some sheep are raised for their meat, but others are bred specifically for their wool, and to get the best from a fleece you need to know something about the various sheep breeds and the characteristics of their wool – the thickness and length of the fibre, the lustre and the crimp. Wool which has lustre, a good wavy crimp and which does not spring back into shape after being squeezed in your hand, is likely to felt well. Wool which is smooth, lacks lustre and has fibres all the same length is probably from a sheep bred for its meat, and is likely to be difficult to felt.

Wool usually comes straight from the sheep in a filthy state, so before it is dyed it needs to be cleaned to remove the dirt and grease, then 'carded' to make all the fibres lie in the same direction in one con-tinuous length. These are skills in their own right, however, and are not vital to the feltmaker although they might be use-ful. We recommend that you start with ready-prepared combed and dyed merino wool 'tops' which can be bought from some craft shops and various mail order suppliers, some of which are listed at the back of this book.

If you have been given a fleece, or have acquired one which you want to store, you should pack it into paper sacks. Do not use plastic bags, especially if the fleece is in its natural state, as stored like this it can become a breeding ground for bacteria and mould. Keep the bags in a cool, dry, airy place, and don't forget to label them with the date, breed of sheep, and any other relevant information. Unwashed wool will discolour and degenerate over time, so try to use it within twelve months. Commercially pre-pared combed and dyed tops can be stored for longer, but do try to avoid unnecessary handling because the coils can begin to felt or toughen and then it can be difficult to pull the fibres apart.

When ordering from a supplier for the first time it may be helpful to know how much fleece you will need, so we give approximate quantities needed for each project.

A fleece is the shorn wool from a sheep. When we use the term 'fleece', it can mean the whole fleece from one sheep or simply a mass of wool fibres. A single strand of wool fibre is covered with tiny scales which vary from coarse to fine, depending on the breed of sheep. Each scale is fixed at one end to the core of the fibre; when pressure and moisture are applied, these scales open, become entangled with each other, and finally lock into position to form a dense mat-felt.

Hand Care

If your skin is likely to suffer from the effects of soap combined with friction and hot water, you will need to experiment with different types of barrier cream and protective gloves. Certainly it is more difficult to learn the feel of the wool as it felts when there are gloves between you and it, but the rolling method (explained later) of feltmaking is perfectly feasible and will reduce the amount of time that your hands are in direct contact with soap and water. You need to take good care of your hands, because rough skin and rag nails will make it difficult to handle the fleece, and this can be frustrating when you are fired up with creativity! A quick and inexpensive skin softener is sugar or salt and olive oil, rubbed well in. Rinse thoroughly, dry carefully, and apply hand cream which should be totally absorbed before handling the fleece.

THE PH FACTOR

The pH scale is used to measure a substance's alkalinity or acidity, over a range from zero to fourteen. A reading of pH7 is neutral, higher than seven indicates an alkaline substance such as soap, and lower than seven is acidic.

Looking at some of the apocryphal stories of how felt was first made, we see that it can be made without using soap; however, at wool's natural pH factor of between three and seven the felting process is slow and the shrinkage of the fabric is lower than when a more acid or an alkaline solution is used, given the same amount of agitation, heat and moisture. An extreme acid or gently alkaline solution helps the elasticity of the fibres, encouraging them to tangle and hold together to form a solid and dense felt.

It is possible to make felt with urine or vinegar, both of which are acidic, but the smell is unpleasant to work with and can be difficult to remove. For this reason you will be glad to know that we have used soap or detergent for all the projects.

Soap is the best alkaline solution to use. You can use any sort of soap: household soap, toilet soap or soap flakes. It also helps to know whether your water supply is hard or soft, and to use a soap that makes a minimum amount of suds. While it is lovely to wallow in the bubbles, soap suds are full of air, and bubbles between the fibres will prevent them matting together and will slow down the speed of felting. When you have completed your feltmaking, you must rinse all traces of soap from the item: if it is left to dry, it can rot the felt fabric. Some people like to give the felt a last rinse in a dilute solution of vinegar to remove every last trace of soap.

3 Beginner's Workshop

FLAT FELT

MATERIALS NEEDED:

- Old towel
- Nylon net at least 62cm (24in) by 31cm (12in) – bigger is fine
- About 50g (2oz) white fleece, and small amounts of various colours
- Optional: wooden slatted blind or beachmat
- Warm water with a few drops of washing-up liquid in it

Begin by laying the towel on the place where you will work. The towel will get very wet, so if the surface happens to be your best dining table you would be well advised to cover it with a large sheet of something waterproof before you begin. Place your net on top of the towel so that half is on the towel and the excess is at the top; you will need to fold the net over when the fleece has been laid out.

Take up the white fleece, holding it in your left hand (if you are left-handed hold it in your right hand) at least 13–15cm (5–6in) from the end; if you hold it too near the end it is very difficult to pull off layers.

With your other hand, put the tips of your fingers under the very ends of the fleece.

Use the tips of the fingers to pull out wisps of wool.

Grasp some fibres with your thumb and fingers, and pull: you should be holding a very fine bunch of fibres of about 10–13cm (4–5in) long.

Do not hold the fleece too near the end.

Opposite: Deborah McGavock, 'Brighton Banner'.

Then lay a third layer with the fibres going in the same way as the first layer.

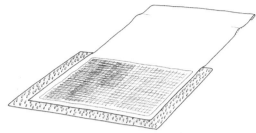

Third layer.

Lay these on the net, then continue to pull more fibres, laying them next to each other until they form a row approximately 30cm (12in) long.

You should now have a very fluffy square of fleece which we are going to use as the 'paper' in our design. It should not have any obviously thin parts, nor should the towel show through anywhere: if it does, put some more fleece on those areas.

Now comes the interesting part: take up the coloured fleece and, using exactly the same technique of pulling the fibres from the large tops, lay out your chosen design. This time the fibres can be laid in any direction so that you are actually 'drawing' with them: mix and match the colours in any way you choose.

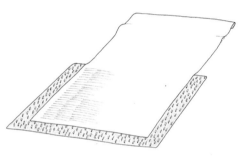

First layer – overlap ends.

Continue pulling out fibres and make another row, laying them all in the same direction and slightly overlapping the ends until you have formed a square of approximately 30sq cm (12sq in).

Now begin the second layer in exactly the same way, but laying the fibres at right angles to the first layer.

Lay on your design.

At this stage you can also lay on other natural fibres in the form of, say, silk caps or embroidery cottons or knitting yarn. Adding natural fibres is easy as they become part of the felt when it is worked;

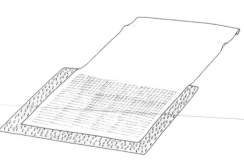

Second layer at right angles.

however, if you add man-made fibres they may not work as well. Thus for this first attempt at felting try to use only natural fibres.

When you are happy with the design, cover it with the other half of the net.

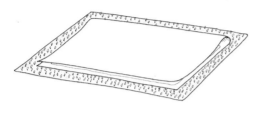

Fold over net.

Now you will need some warm water in a jug. If you are going to use washing-up liquid, add only a drop or two to the water: it really does not need very much, so make sure it is just a drop. You can always add more if you feel it isn't quite enough, but too much will make your felt very soapy and slimy to work on. Place one hand on top of the net with the fingers spread wide, and pour the water down onto your hand first so that it doesn't disturb your design if it falls in a sudden rush.

Pour the water gently.

Go over the whole surface of your felt so that it is wet through; you may have to push the water down through the fibres by pressing flat with your hand. When the bundle is all wet, start rubbing the surface of the net gently with a circular motion until all the area with wool underneath is

flat. Do not be too vigorous at this stage as you will move your design. Use sufficient pressure to produce a little friction on the fibres, but not so much as to move the whole bundle. You will notice that the pile of fibres starts to become flattened as you work around the net.

Rub the whole surface.

It is not a good idea to wear rubber gloves at this stage as they pull lots of the fibre through the net. However, if you prefer to keep your hands out of the wet for as long as possible, then protect them whilst you do the rubbing by putting them in clear plastic bags.

When the whole area is flat – which can take anything from only a few minutes to fifteen – turn the whole bundle over in its net and repeat the wetting and rubbing on the back. Then turn back to the original side and start to lift the net: do this gently. If it is sticking to the felt, lift the whole thing by pulling gently, looking at the design all the while to make sure it is not being pulled out of shape. When the fibres have become flat and are holding together enough to lift as a piece of fabric, this is known as a half-felt or a pre-felt.

Cover it again with the net, and rub some more: this process can be continued, on back and front, until the fibres are no longer coming up from the surface of your picture when pulled between finger and thumb. This process alone will make you your felt, but if you have a beachmat or a wooden slatted blind you can hurry the felting along a bit by rolling the whole net-covered piece into the mat or blind,

Whenever you make a piece, note how many layers you have used, and how much the felt has shrunk: these can be important factors as you go on to more adventurous projects, and will determine its finished look and strength. For instance, a felt that is going to be used as a decorative item will need to be only softly felted, and will not need to be fulled as much as one that is going to be worn, or used as a bag.

then rolling it back and fore like a rolling pin. Remember to look at the felt now and again to make sure that the net is still coming away from the surface.

Once the pattern is holding firmly to the background white fleece, you can remove the net altogether and either rub it or roll it in the mat or blind until the felt becomes firm and 'hard'. It is very difficult to describe this state exactly, but you will notice a difference in the feel of the fabric. This is known as the 'fulling' process.

When you think the felt is hard, rinse the whole piece under both hot and cold water to remove all the soap or detergent; this should also reveal whether it needs more rolling or rubbing to harden it more. At this stage you can rub it against itself: this is another way of 'fulling'. In fact you can do any of the things you would avoid doing to your best woollens when you wash them, as all these things help the felt become as hard as possible.

Your picture should now have shrunk quite a bit, and it may be aquiring some ripples across its surface: this is a sign that it is finished. You should rinse and dry the piece thoroughly, as any soap left in the fabric can lead to rotting. Some feltmakers recommend adding a drop of vinegar to the final rinse to help make the wool mothproof. It can be ironed, as can any other wool item, if required.

If by now you have discovered that you like felting, and if you can immediately think of another picture that you would like to make, then like us, you are well on the way to being addicted. In this case we suggest you try making a few more flat pieces so that you become familiar with the technique, and learn to recognize how soon you can stop using the net, and how soon you can start to roll up the felt in a mat to speed up the felting process.

There are many ways of making felt, and with practice you will find your own favourite. Some people never rub at all, but go straight to the rolling method; others use bubble wrap instead of net: they lay the fibres on one layer of wrap, sprinkle with water and soap, then cover with another piece of wrap and with wet and soapy hands, rub the top surface of this layer. We have heard of people using a flat-bed sander to do the rubbing, with the flat surface covered in smooth rubber – though if you do this, bear in mind the risks inherent in using electricity in association with water, and be sure to take every precaution. Some have even invented machines to make large pieces of felt which would take a long time to produce entirely by hand.

ROLLS OF FELT

Next we will learn how to make rolls of felt, used for bag handles, buttons, jewellery or decorative items.

MATERIALS NEEDED

◆ Towel
◆ Beachmat or wooden blind
◆ Small amounts of fleece

A very simple, small roll can be made by breaking off a piece of wool top about 30cm (12in) long, and then dividing it in two, lengthways.

If you wind a thin piece of a different colour around the outside you will create a striped roll.

If there are lots of suds, rinse some off and then continue.

Now, lay the fleece on the beachmat or blind. Wet and soap the hands, sprinkle the fleece with water, and then roll it back and fore just as you would if you were making a coil in pottery or a sausage shape in playdough...

Alternatively a good way is to pick up the fleece and roll it between your hands, because the warmth from your hands will help it to felt.

...doing this on the rough surface of the blind makes it felt more quickly.

Keep rolling until it becomes hard and shrunk, then rinse thoroughly, and dry.

Once you have mastered the technique, practise making different lengths and thicknesses. Also, if you use the technique of laying out the fleece on a mat, try using different coloured layers, because when rolled up these will give a coloured pattern through the centre like a stick of rock.

BALLS OF FELT

These can be made in all sizes, and are used for decorations, earrings, buttons, toys and necklaces.

MATERIALS NEEDED

- Small amounts of fleece
- Beachmat (though this is optional)

Start by scrunching up some small pieces of fleece into a round shape.

Pull layers of fleece from the tops, as you do when making flat felt, and progressively wrap the shape with thin layers of fleece. Place the layers on the ball in different directions, in the same way that a ball of knitting wool is wound.

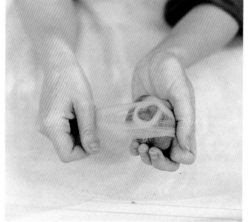

You will need to keep layering until the ball is quite large, as all the air trapped within it means that it will inevitably shrink a lot when felted.

For this first try, make it about the size of a tennis ball, or until it is a comfortable shape to hold in your hands.

Next, sprinkle the ball with water, and then wet and soap your hands. Keeping the hands cupped, move the ball around in your palms in a circular motion. Be careful not to put any pressure on it at this stage: just keep the hands loosely cupped and let it find its own level. If you apply too much pressure at this stage the felt will form into folds, and these are difficult to remove. Add more water if it feels too dry.

Keep circling the hands until the ball has shrunk and feels hard when squeezed: by this stage it should be about 2.5cm (1in) in diameter.

Rinse thoroughly, squeezing hard to remove all traces of soap, then dry.

These balls can be made with different coloured layers so that when they are cut open the different colours are revealed.

Now that you have tried out these three very basic methods you are clearly ready to make them up into something: we have therefore devised the following simple items for you to try first.

CHRISTMAS DECORATIONS

Christmas Angel

MATERIALS NEEDED

- 30g (1oz) white fleece
- Net
- Some coloured fleece or knitting wool for hair

First make a flat piece of white felt using the instructions already given. If you lay out a 30cm (12in) square of fleece you should have plenty. While that is drying, make a small ball of felt using either all white fleece or with the top few layers a flesh colour of your choice; this will be the angel's head. The finished ball should be about 2cm (¾in) in diameter. Rinse well, then allow to dry.

Following the pattern below, cut out the angel body from your flat piece of felt; also cut a strip of felt about 3.5 cm (1.5in) wide and 10cm (4in) long. This will be used to make the arms of your angel.

Make a ball for the head and attach it firmly to the top of the cone, using a few good stitches.

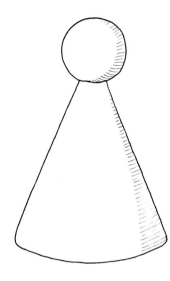

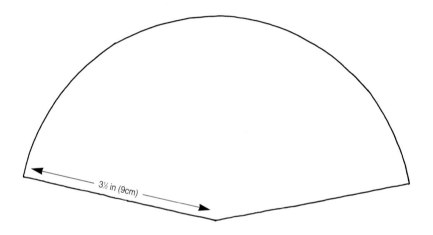

3½ in (9cm)

Now take the strip of white felt and roll it along its length to form the arm shape: attach one end to the centre back of the angel, then bring the arm round to the front of the angel's body, using a few stitches to hold it in place.

Fold the body pattern so that the straight edges abut each other and it forms a cone shape; then hand-stitch the edges almost to the top.

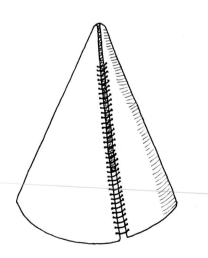

back…

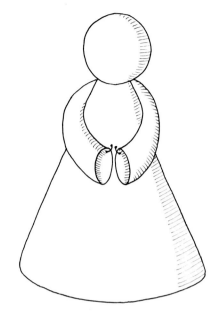

...and front.

You can make wings out of netting or lace, cutting them to shape and stitching them just below the arms at the centre back.

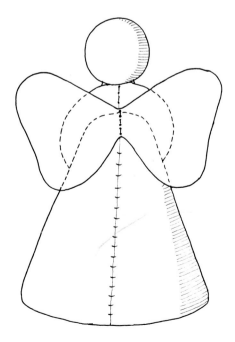

The hair on our sample is made with some Wensleydale wool dyed yellow, but you could equally well use embroidery thread or knitting wool. To hold it in place, either stitch it down the middle from front to back so that the stitches look like a central parting, or use felting needles to attach fleece to head.

For the last tiny details we have taken some gold-coloured craft wire and bent it into shape to make a miniscule tiara – only if you wish – and a leaf decoration. Alternatively you could use a sequin candle for your angel to hold, or a bead.

Wreath decoration

MATERIALS NEEDED

◆ 25g (1oz) fleece

For this you would need to make two long rolls of felt about 38cm (15in) in length, and about ½cm (¼in) in diameter – one in red and one in green would give a good effect.

Break off a piece of wool top about 38cm (15in) long, then divide it into two down its length. Wet and roll this between your hands or on a mat until it is hard and shrunk. Rinse well. Repeat with a second colour, and leave both until they are dry. Then stitch both together at one end and twist them along their length.

Form this twisted roll into a circle, finishing off neatly – you may need to cut it.

Disguise the join by cutting tiny holly leaves from a small piece of green flat felt, or some fabric or paper, and stitching

these to the wreath. You might also add some red beads for berries, or perhaps tiny balls of felt.

Icicle decoration

MATERIALS NEEDED

- 10g (½oz) fleece
- Gold braid

This is one of the simplest decorations to make, but when you have lots of them hanging on your tree the effect is stunning.

Start by breaking off a piece of wool top about 15cm (6in) long, then pull it into three pieces along its length. Wet these, then roll them between the hands until they start to felt; fold a little of the fleece back onto itself at one end to form a slightly thicker part. Continue rolling until the pieces have hardened and shrunk; note that putting more pressure on the felt at one end will make it into a pointed shape. Rinse well and allow to dry.

Take up some gold- or silver-coloured trimming: stitch one end of it at the bottom of the icicle to anchor it, then wind it around the felt, stitching it as and when necessary to hold it in place.

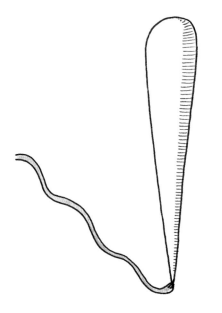

Star decoration

EQUIPMENT NEEDED:

- 25g (1oz) white fleece
- White net
- Coloured sequins

For this project you need some flat white felt about 20 × 12.75cm (8 × 5in).

Cut out two identical star shapes and remove the centres, leaving about 1.25cm (½in) felt all round. Next, cut two pieces of white net – the sort used for ballerina tutus or stiff petticoats – slightly bigger than the felt stars. Now make a sandwich of felt star, net, coloured sequins, net and the second felt star, then stitch round the edge making sure you go through all the layers; an easy way to do this is with a sewing machine using the zigzag stitch. Trim away the excess net, and finally attach a looped thread to one point to hang it up by.

Make the top end into a loop for hanging the icicle on the tree, stitching it to hold it firm.

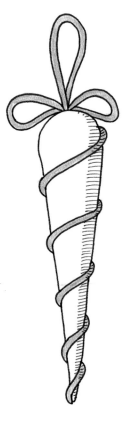

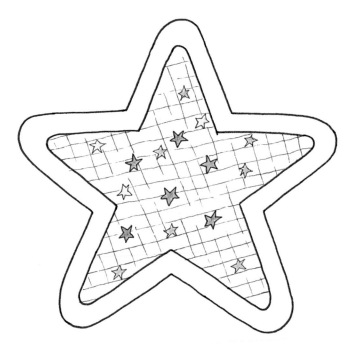

Heart decoration

MATERIALS NEEDED:

- 20g (1oz) fleece
- Optional gold fabric
- Gold braid

For this project you will need some small pieces of flat felt, in two colours; we used red and white. Alternatively you could use felt in one colour and gold fabric. You will also need a large and a small heart pattern. Cut two large-size hearts from the felt, and then cut two small-size hearts from either the gold fabric or the different coloured felt.

(Right) Sew loop of ribbon between the two halves.

with any shape – for instance egg shapes at Easter, Christmas trees at Christmas time.

Stitch the small hearts to the larger ones at their centres. Decorate the pieces with embroidery or beads if you want. Put the two large-size hearts wrong sides together, and stitch neatly round the edge to secure; before you finish at the top, slip a loop of ribbon between the two halves and stitch into place, to hang your decoration up by.

Sew gold braid all round the edges of the hearts. The decoration is now reversible. You can, of course, do this

(Below right) Attach gold braid.

We are sure that you will find many other ways to make decorations once you start to make felt. For instance, scraps of flat felt can be used to make greetings cards: cut Christmas tree shapes from scraps of green felt and decorate with sequins, then attach to a card background. Small fish and butterflies also make good subjects to attach to cards. None of your felt need be wasted.

JEWELLERY

Making jewellery utilizes the felt-making techniques we have already discussed: for instance, small pieces of flat felt, balls and rolls are used to make earrings.

Leaf-shape earrings

MATERIALS NEEDED:

- ◆ Two small pieces of small-gauge bubble wrap
- ◆ Fleece in the colour of your choice
- ◆ Earring hooks

For this project you will need to make some flat felt first. Lay an old towel on your work surface, to mop up any water; then lay one piece of bubble wrap on the towel, with the bubbles uppermost. Pull out your fleece into thin layers to form a small square of about 15cm (6in) – this

A selection of earrings.

quantity will in fact make more than one pair of earrings. Three layers is usually adequate as earrings need to be light, and more will risk making them too heavy. Using a different colour for each layer can give a very interesting effect.

Next, sprinkle the fleece with some water mixed with washing-up liquid or soap flakes, then cover with the second piece of bubble wrap, bubble side down. Wet your hand and start to rub all over the outside of the bubble wrap. Turn over and repeat on the other side.

After a while check your layers of fleece to make sure that all is wet enough and forming into a felt; continue until it is holding firm. To finish the fulling process, remove from the bubble wrap and rub between your hands.

Cut out the shapes that you want for your earrings, then rub these some more between the bubble wrap to smooth off the cut edges. Rinse and dry.

Embroider the felt if you wish; alternatively just attach the findings.

Spirals

For spirals you need the sort of finding onto which beads are threaded, namely a small piece of silver wire with one end rolled into a circle to stop the beads falling off; when making earrings we will use that end for attaching to the earring hook. To make the spiral, cover the straight part with some fleece. You need very small amounts of fleece for this, and it is best felted by rubbing directly in your hand using just two fingers of the other hand. Then rinse and dry as usual. Twist into a spiral shape.

Balls

Balls for jewellery are made following the technique already described on pp. 27–28.

They may then be threaded onto the straight silver bead findings described in 'Spirals' above, with the rolled end used as a stop; or simply thread them through with some shiny thread, and then tie this to the hook.

CUSHION COVER

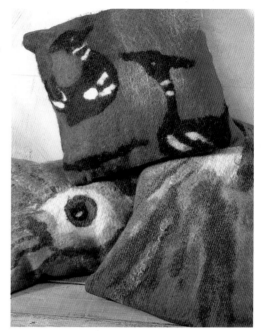

(Right) Three cushions by Deborah McGavock.

One of the advantages of using home-made felt for your cushion covers is that you can design them to match the existing decor – you might even choose to incorporate a particular feature or element of the room into your design. In any event, you will have very individual cushions.

A piece of felt that is intended for use as a cushion cover must always be very well fulled – you could even put the finished piece through a wool wash cycle in the washing machine to make sure it is quite hard and not likely to shrink any further when it is washed after it has been made up. Remember to allow for all this shrinking when you are laying out the fleece.

MATERIALS NEEDED

- Cushion pad
- Flat piece of felt the size of the cushion pad, plus 2.5cm (1in) all round
- Fabric for the back of the cushion cover (this could be more felt)
- If your cushion pad is 45cm^2 (18sq in) the fabric or felt needed for the back will be two pieces both measuring 48 × 30cm (19 × 12in)
- Three buttons

Begin with the pieces for the back: turn over 6mm (¼in) in a hem down one 48cm (19in) side of each piece of fabric – these two will eventually be buttoned together to form the centre back. Machine stitch close to the edge on both pieces.

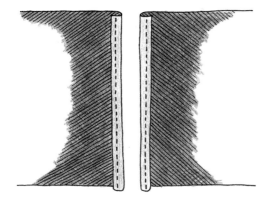

On one piece turn over another 2.5cm (1in) in a hem, and stitch through all the layers; you can machine stitch if you prefer. On the other piece make a 5cm (2in) hem and hand stitch in place.

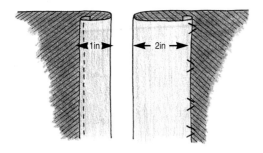

On the right side of the piece with the 2.5cm (1in) turning, attach three buttons: stitch the first in the centre and the other two 15cm (6in) away from the first. Make buttonholes in the other piece of fabric to match the positions of the buttons on the first piece.

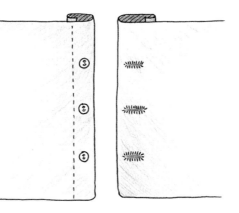

The buttonholes can be machine made or hand-stitched. Next, button the two back pieces together, then place the back and the front pieces of the cushion cover together with the right sides facing.

Machine stitch around the outside, 13mm (½in) in from the edge all round. Trim the excess material from the corners with a diagonal cut.

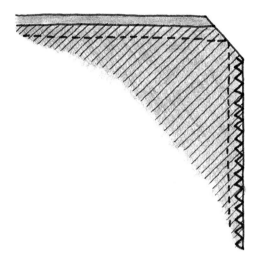

MATERIALS NEEDED

◆ Large flat piece of ready-made felt, enough to cut out two fronts made with about 75g (3oz) of the main colour for a child's; 100g (4oz) for an adult's
◆ Approximately 75cm (30in) of fabric suitable for the waistcoat back
◆ Approximately 1m (39in) of fabric for the waistcoat lining
◆ Two or three buttons or balls of felt
◆ Pattern for the waistcoat

First, cut out all the pattern pieces for the two front pieces, the back and the lining pieces. With the right sides together, join the front pieces to the back piece at the shoulder seams.

Neaten the edges with machine zigzag stitch, or blanket stitch by hand. Then unfasten the buttons, and turn the cover right sides out. Pull the corners into shape, and finally insert the pad.

(Far right) Join shoulder seams.

WAISTCOAT

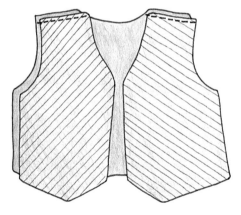

Do the same with the lining pieces. Press the seams open at the shoulders.

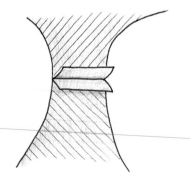

Child's waistcoat.

(Far right) Press seams open.

Next, sew the lining to the waistcoat: do this by putting the right sides together, then sew together all around the edges, leaving the side seams unstitched.

Trim any excess seam allowance; to help the seam curve round the neck, snip half a dozen times or so at right angles into the seam allowance, being careful not to cut through the seam stitching itself.

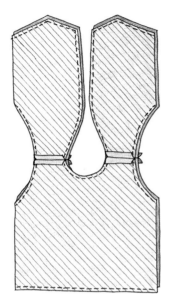

Leave side seams unstitched.

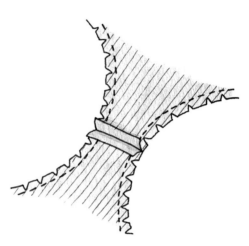

Snip into curves.

The child's blue spotted waistcoat is made in the same way, except we also made some thin rolls of felt as fringes for the fronts. These and the cord loops are pinned and stitched in place before the lining is attached.

Insert a hand into the centre of the waistcoat through the back side-seam opening, and pull the fronts up through the shoulder seams so that the right sides are now outside. Note that both fronts must be pulled out through one side seam so that the garment may be turned completely.

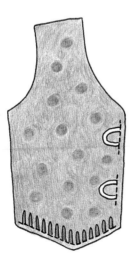

Attach loops and fringe first, to right side of front.

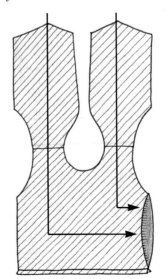

Pull fronts through shoulders and out one side.

Press flat. With the right sides together, stitch along the side seams through three layers of fabric.

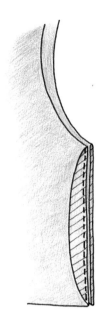

Join side seams through three layers.

Trim off any excess, then fold the seam allowance of the lining under and hand stitch so as to enclose all the seams.

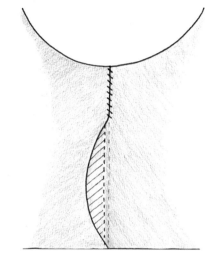

Hand stitch to finish.

If you wish to topstitch around all the edges, this is the time to do it. Finally, sew on buttons and make buttonholes to match.

Needle-Punched Felt

Hand-made felt takes time and a great deal of energy, but there is an easier way: needle-punching. This involves the rapid, repeated punching of barbed needles into a web of fleece, entangling the fibres to form felt. For those who still want the hands-on approach, or who want to felt a stubborn area, it is possible to buy a small hand-punching tool with either a single needle or six needles (*see* Suppliers). The single needle is useful for attaching fine details, or for shaping a solid piece of felt with contours; the six-needle tool is used to tack details onto your dry fleece before felting. The needles must be used with care as they are very sharp. It takes practice to use them without breaking them, but they are helpful.

If, however, you dream of making a really huge felt, then visit Huddersfield University in Yorkshire and learn to use the needle-punching machine there: its needle board has over 1,000 needles. With this machine you can make 1m (39in) of felt in just ten minutes, which leaves you free to concentrate on design. You can then put the same length of felt through the machine again, this time adding any other textile fibre which will be felted in. Obviously this sort of machine is for industrial use, primarily for making such utilitarian items as car carpets, carpet tiles and insulation material; however, they are becoming more widely used by the fashion industry for coats and jackets, for which purpose the design potential is enormous.

GALLERY PHOTOS

Jeanette Appleton, 'Islands 1', hand-made felt, stitched and slashed in parts (142 x 76cm).

Roswitha Howells,
hand-made felt.

Christine Lewis, 'Spirit in the Sky', felt with machine embroidery.

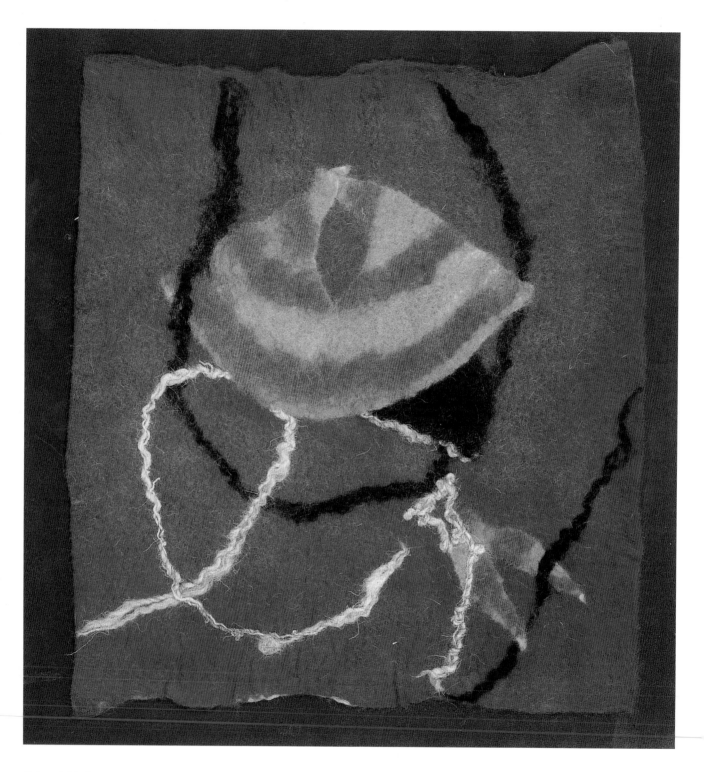

Deborah McGavock, 'Stolen'.

4 Intermediate Workshop

USING A RESIST IN FELTMAKING

Those of you who know about dyeing, or watercolour painting or printmaking will think of a resist as a way of preventing colour getting to a certain part or parts of your work. In feltmaking, however, it is used to stop the fleece felting to itself when making a three-dimensional object using the flat rolling method. The resist can be made with any heavy-duty plastic: this might be builders' plastic; or the bags that garden sand comes in; or bubble wrap, the sort with the small bubbles giving the best surface to work with; or it could be the foam-type wrapping that electrical items are sometimes packed in. Even the polystyrene base from oven-ready pizzas could be cut up and used, though bear in mind that it is difficult to roll up in a mat and so lends itself best to the flat rubbing method.

Using this method of placing a plastic resist between the layers of fleece enables you to make a variety of shapes which have seams, but without involving you in any sewing. It is quite tricky to master at first, however, and we would suggest that before you try it, you should make quite a few pieces of flat felt, balls and rolls so that you know how many layers of fleece you need in order to achieve the thickness you want. You should also know how the fleece reacts when you wet it, and when the felt has formed a 'skin' and is ready to have the resist removed. Nevertheless it is a very useful method of working, and we are sure that once you have tried it a few times, you will then continue to use it often. It is the basis for all sorts of items such as slippers, bags, hats and even clothing once you have mastered the technique.

Purse, mule and baby boot

SIMPLE PURSE WITH A FLAP

MATERIALS NEEDED

◈ Towel
◈ Net
◈ Beachmat or window blind
◈ Approximately 40g (2oz) fleece in a chosen colour
◈ Piece of A4-size paper
◈ Piece of heavy-duty plastic, or bubble wrap cut to A5 size
◈ Soap and water

Lay the towel on the table, and the mat on top of this if you are using one. Lay out the net and put down the piece of A4 paper on the net.

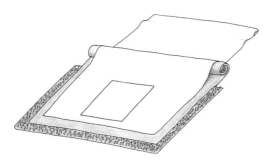

Using your chosen colour of fleece, pull out and make a layer to cover the size of the paper. Lay down more layers, each one in the opposite direction from the one before, until you have the thickness you want. We used four layers. Now lay two more layers on one half only of the pile. This area will form the flap of the purse.

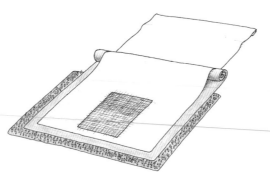

Four layers to cover A4 size.

Put the plastic pattern piece onto the half of the pile that has the fewest layers, leaving an even margin all round the edges. The pattern piece will reach slightly more than half way, and will therefore cover just a little of the half with six layers of fleece.

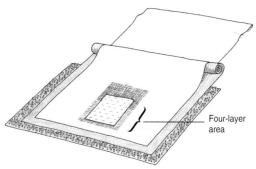

Four-layer area

The pattern piece placed over the four-layer area.

Lay down four more layers of fleece over the plastic, with the edges matching the under-layers but leaving the top part of the plastic peeping out to show where the six-layer part begins.

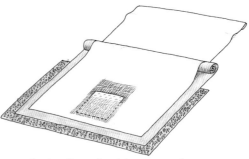

Leave the top 2cm of resist uncovered.

Tidy the edges as much as possible by tucking the feathery ends under. Then carefully slide the piece of A4 paper out from under the pile of fleece.

Cover with net. If you want, you can fold the net so that it forms a fold at the point where the edge of the fleece is laid; this will keep the edges neater when you are working.

Wet, and begin to felt as usual, either by rubbing with your hands or by rolling in the beachmat. It is important to remember to turn the whole package over and wet the other side, because the plastic in the middle will of course stop the water getting through all the layers. It will feel puffy until it has become thoroughly wet.

Rub for a short while, then open up the net and reshape the edges, if necessary, by folding neatly under or over. Then re-cover with the net and continue the felting process until the felt has formed a skin. Remove the net: the areas which did not have the plastic resist will have joined together forming a seamed area around the edges of the purse. Where the plastic was inserted is now a pouch, namely the inside of the purse.

Before you take the plastic out, place the felt flat, put your hand on top of the plastic between the layers, and start to rub over this area as it will not have received any attention while it was in the net. Turn the purse over so that you can do this on both the inside surfaces. When you are satisfied that this area has also formed a skin you can remove the plastic to see how your purse is forming. You may need to tidy up the edges by folding over or trimming with sharp scissors at this stage, then continue to felt by rubbing or rolling until it starts to harden; the felt will shrink and become harder the more you work it. When you are satisfied that it will shrink no further, rinse and dry the purse.

For the purse in the picture we have made a roll of felt which has been stitched into place as a covering for the snap fastener.

If you wish to have a design on the back and top flap of your purse, this should be the first thing to be laid on the A4 sheet of paper at the dry stage.

If you wish to fashion different shapes of flap you can cut into the top half of the purse at the skin or half-felt stage, or you can shape it as you lay the fleece. The plastic resist can obviously be any shape you wish.

Experiment so that in the future you can make any shape you want.

RESIST USING A BALL

This is a fun project in which you can see how the resist method – this time using a rubber ball – would look without seams such as the purse has. This is a good project to do with children.

MATERIALS NEEDED

- Approximately 20g (1oz) fleece
- Plastic ball the size of a tennis ball (if you only have a tennis ball then wrap it completely in cling film)
- Old pair of tights or a piece of net
- Water and soap

Start by covering the ball with thin layers of fleece, changing direction with each layer as you would when you wind up a ball of knitting yarn.

Continue making layers until the ball seems quite large; make sure that you cannot see any part of its surface through the layers.

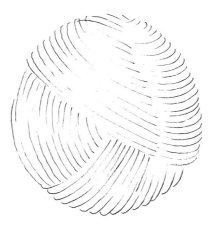

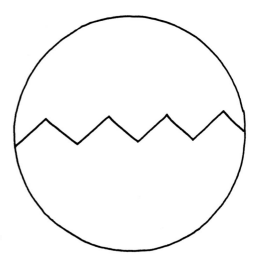

Take up the pair of tights, and cut off one of the legs close to where it joins the body. Tie a knot in the foot part of the cut-off leg, then carefully put the fleece-covered ball into the leg part.

Now wet the ball through the tights, and wet your hands and soap them. Start rubbing the ball all over with your soapy hands; you may need to add more water as you go along. The ball will form some wrinkles at first, but carry on rubbing and they should disappear.

Keep rubbing until the felt has formed and become quite firm; then remove the pair of tights and rub the ball again until it is quite smooth. Using a pair of sharp, pointed scissors, you can now cut through the layers of fleece in order to remove the ball. Where and how you make the cuts will determine what your finished piece looks like: for instance, if you want a single pot shape, make two cuts in a cross at one point, and no bigger than necessary to get the ball out.

Or you could cut the whole thing in half around the middle, making two half cups: these might be used for flower-type decorations – cutting a zigzag line round the centre will enhance this petal effect.

Once you have removed the ball, the inside surfaces of the felt will need more rubbing to firm them up before you rinse and dry them.

BAG WITH LOOPS

MATERIALS NEEDED

- Towel
- Net
- Beachmat or blind
- Approximately 100g (3½oz) of the main colour fleece
- Coloured fleece for decoration
- Square of plastic for resist, 35cm (14in) square
- Four 7.5cm (3in) lengths of piping cord
- 1.5m (5ft) of thick cotton rope for the handles

Start by making the four loops which are to hold the rope handle in place: the four short pieces of piping cord will each form the centre of a roll of felt.

Cover dry ends of loops with more layers.

With your towel and mat on the table as before, lay out four rectangles of fleece approximately 7.5 × 15cm (3 × 6in) to a thickness of four layers. Put a short length of piping cord onto each one, and roll up to cover completely.

Now wet the centre section of each roll, and rub just this area; keep the edges of the rolls as dry as possible because you can then add these to the bag layers at a later stage.

Leave dry fleece at ends.

Keep felting these centre sections until they are well fulled and hard; however, do not rinse these pieces yet. Put to one side while you start the bag.

Lay the net on top of the beachmat or blind, and start to make layers of the main colour fleece; these should be approximately 38 × 38cm (15 × 15in). When you have done two layers, form the rolls into loop shapes and spread the dry areas of fleece at the ends onto the bag fleece at the top.

Put a further two layers of fleece on top of these so that the loops are now buried in the centre layers of fleece.

Put your piece of resist on top of this so that one edge is level with the top of the bag; fleece should overhang the other three edges.

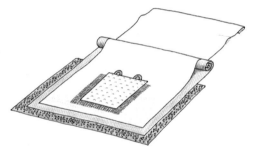

Now comes the tricky bit: fold the overlapping edges onto the top side of the piece of plastic – if they slip off, then spray the plastic with water or wet the edges of the fleece.

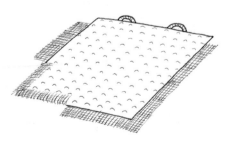

Pull out another layer of fleece to reach just to the edges of the plastic, and then lay a second layer in the opposite direction so that it overlaps the edges of the resist by about 13mm (½in). Now place two more loops into position at the top edge of the bag. Cover with two more layers of fleece, each slightly overlapping the previous layers by about 13mm (½in) on the three sides of the bag.

If you want to add a design to the bag that can be done now.

Cover with the net, then lift the whole package and turn it over, and gently lift the net on this side. Now fold the overlapping fleece from the other side onto this side again, neatening up the edges. Cover again with the net, and felt as usual by wetting and rubbing, or rolling in the mat until a skin is formed on the felt.

Open up the package to check that the edges are still in a good shape. Adjust if necessary, then cover up again and continue rolling until the fabric has shrunk sufficiently to fit the resist.

Open up, remove the resist, and turn the whole bag inside out. At this stage you will be able to see if unsightly thick ridges have formed near the side seams. If they have, stretch them gently until they lie flat again. Check that the top edges of the bag are forming nicely, and that the loops are holding in place.

Roll up in the mat again so that you can full the inside part of the felt which was previously against the plastic and not benefiting from the friction. As soon as all the felt has formed into a half felt or skin you can rub it against itself, which will help it to full more quickly. Pay particular attention to where the loops are joined in, as this must be well fulled to make it strong.

Rinse, and check again to see that whole bag is shrinking and fulling evenly. Continue to roll and rub if necessary. When the felt is hard and the bag is very strong, give a final rinse and leave to dry. Then cut the rope into two pieces and thread through the loops, tying knots in the ends to stop it slipping through.

SIMPLE FROG GLOVE PUPPET

Frog and witch puppets.

You can also make glove puppets using the resist method. Below are instructions for making a simple frog glove puppet, though with practice you will be able to make puppets that are as complicated as you like. (For instance, the more complicated witch puppet is made by combining this resist method with felting over foam; instructions for this are given later in the book, see p. 70.)

MATERIALS NEEDED

- Towel
- Beachmat
- Pattern cut from strong plastic or bubble wrap
- Approximately 40g (2oz) green fleece
- Small amount of white felt for eyes

Make a pattern by drawing round an adult hand and cut out 5cm (2in) bigger all round. Lay the towel on the table and the beachmat on top, then the net on top of that. Place the pattern on the net and lay down green fleece in layers as usual. For this shape we find it is best to lay the fleece diagonally across the body of the puppet, because the thumb and finger parts can then be made more easily. Over-

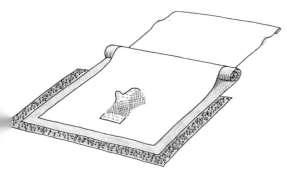

lap the edges of the pattern slightly more with each successive layer.

Four layers should be plenty. Next, slide one hand under the bubble wrap and put the other hand on top of the fleece layers, and turn the whole thing over so that the fleece is underneath and the pattern shape on top. Now turn the overlapping fleece over onto the bubble wrap, keeping the edges close to the pattern. Wet if necessary, to hold in place. Make four more layers of green fleece as before.

Turn the whole thing over once more, and fold over the extra fleece from the edges. Cover with net, and wet and felt as previously. When both sides are wet and lying flat against the pattern, roll up in the mat to help firm it up.

Take off the net and make sure that the edges are not forming flat seams, as this time we do not want any ridges along the sides. If they are, fold over onto the pattern piece again, cover once more with net, and continue rolling until a skin is formed and the felt is holding in shape.

Next, uncover and slide a hand between one layer of the puppet and the

bubble wrap, and rub the inside surface; then turn over to work the other side. When all is firm, remove the resist and turn the whole puppet inside out. If there are any large ridges on the sides, stretch the fabric over the back of your hand and refelt to smooth it out. Make sure you can get your fingers and thumb into the puppet arms. Rub the outside of the felt with one hand whilst your other hand is inside the body of the puppet.

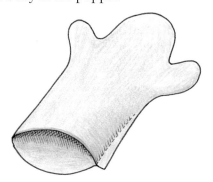

Avoid forming seams.

Keep rolling and rinsing until the felt is very hard and shrunk. Then rinse and leave to dry.

Meanwhile make two small balls of white fleece and felt for the eyes; you may also want to make a very small piece of flat green felt for eyelids. Rinse all these, and leave to dry. Then stitch the eyes in place – if you want, you could cover the back half with small half-circles of flat green felt.

Your frog is now ready for the princess to come along and kiss him.

MULE-TYPE SLIPPER

MATERIALS NEEDED

- Towel
- Beachmat or blind
- Net
- Approximately 120g (5oz) fleece
- Resist patterns for both feet
- Scissors

Begin as usual by laying the towel on the table with the mat on top, and then the net. To make the patterns you will need to draw around the outline of each of your feet onto a piece of paper; then using bubble pack or stiff plastic sheet, cut out the resist pattern, allowing it to be at least 7½cm (3in) bigger than your foot all round. It is always best to make both slippers at the same time, to be sure that each one fits each foot correctly.

Place the resist patterns on the net, being sure that the patterns are the correct way round to make a pair, and start to layer with fleece. We used six layers, and allowed them to overlap the edges of the pattern, each one a little bit more than its predecessor.

Now place one hand beneath the plastic pattern and one on top of the fleece you have laid up, and turn the whole thing over so that the resist now lies on top of the fleece.

If you want your mules to have a design on the fronts you can now lay this directly onto the resist sheet. Spray with water if it will not hold in place.

Next, fold over the overlapping edges of the fleece so that it fits the shape of your pattern tightly.

Now lay down four more layers of fleece to cover this side of the pattern. On the top layer place a small piece of a different coloured fleece over the front part of the slipper: this will be its top. It is essential to do this if you have made a design on your mules, otherwise the patterns could finish up on the sole!

Tuck all the overlapping fleece under so that the edges fit your pattern tightly. Cover with net and start to felt by applying water and rubbing by hand; then turn the slippers over and repeat on the other side.

When the felt has reached the half-felt stage, peel off the net; have the side with the different coloured mark facing upwards. Then, using a pair of sharp scissors, carefully cut through to the point where the pattern widens to become the toe covering, though only as far as the resist.

Cutting in a slight curve will give a better shape to your mule front.

Now, pull out the back part of the resist through the cut, so that the pattern now sits on top of the fleece at the heel part of your mules. Leave the resist in the middle of the front part of the mules.

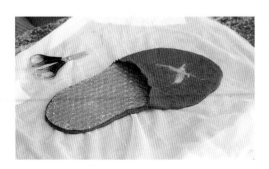

Cover with net again, and carry on felting either by hand or by rolling in the mat. When the felt feels quite firm, remove the net and resist, and turn the slipper inside out so that any design you laid on the fleece now shows on the toes of your slippers. You should now be able to see the shape of your mule forming correctly.

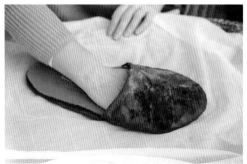

If ridges are forming at the seams, stretch these out so that the felt is flat again. Now continue to full until the mules have shrunk to the correct size and are really firm and strong. We find that rinsing in hot water between rollings helps to speed up this process. Any unsightly lumps and bumps which have appeared along the sole edges can be trimmed and fulled again if necessary.

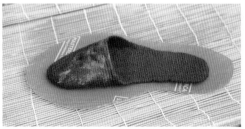

BABY BOOTS

Boots and slippers can also be made with the resist method; we use a pattern which is a sideways view of a boot. Again you must allow a substantial amount for shrinkage – indeed, the pattern for adult-size boots using this method looks as if they will be big enough to fit an elephant; but persevere because they do shrink to shape.

Here we give instructions for a pair of baby boots, but you can make your own patterns for any size you wish. You can also add all sorts of fancy bits such as wings or small baubles of felt using the other methods of feltmaking you have practised.

MATERIALS NEEDED

- Towel
- Beachmat or blind
- Net
- Approximately 80g (3oz) fleece
- Resist patterns for both feet
- Scissors

Using the same principles of resist felt-making as for the purse, bags and slippers, cover your boot pattern with about five layers of fleece and felt to half-felt stage; at this point turn inside out to check that seams are not forming. Then continue until the felt is starting to firm up and shrink.

Decide what sort of opening you would like to have in the boots, and cut accordingly. For the small white boots shown at the beginning of this section we cut into both sides to form a small tongue, and then refelted to smooth the edges of the cuts. When they were quite finished we used some plaited knitting wool to form a loop fastening.

You could also make slippers and boots from flat felt and a moccasin pattern. A professional bootmaker may be able to stitch a proper sole to the bottom of your slippers, which would make them very hard wearing.

Bags by Deborah Roberts and Christine Lewis.

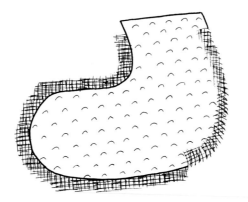

Opposite: Helen Towell, fantastic birds made using the resist method.

5 Expert Workshop

Next we shall make very fine or cobweb felt and also applied felt, and although the same basic equipment is used for these, slightly different methods are involved. A wooden blind is definitely needed, and if you have to buy one, buy the biggest you can find, one you can lay out flat wherever you will be making up the felts.

COBWEB FELT SCARF

MATERIALS NEEDED

- Large wooden blind
- Large piece of net
- 25–40g (2–3oz) fleece

First decide whether you are going to make a square scarf, or a long thin one: for the latter you will need a mat at least 1.5m (5ft) long, and for a square scarf, one about 1.25 × 1.25m (4 × 4ft). It will not matter if the mats are larger than these sizes, but if they are smaller, your finished item will be too small for use.

This time you will need first of all to lay the mat out flat on a waterproof surface. If you do not have a table surface that is suitable perhaps you could use the kitchen floor, though this is not so comfortable for the laying out part. If it is fine and not windy you could work outside. Now lay the net on top of the mat; your net should be 150cm (60in) long by about 60cm (24in) wide.

For a long thin scarf you will need to pull out a very thin layer of fleece down the centre of your net – in fact it must be so fine that you can barely see there is a complete layer. Then make a second layer, again extremely fine, in the opposite direction. You can make each layer a different colour if you wish, as all the colours will be seen in the finished item, or you could mix colours in each layer. Now make a third, very fine layer in the same direction as the first one; you should still be able to see through the three layers, although there should not be any obvious, gaping holes.

Fold the net over from both sides, very close to the edges of your scarf as this will help to form a good edge.

Now you will need a jug of water into which you have dissolved some soap flakes or washing-up liquid; this can be hot or cold, though we find that hot water starts the fleece felting more quickly. Pour it over the fleece in the net and pat it down with your hands to make sure the layers get wet all the way through.

When the whole scarf area is wet, roll up the mat to enclose the scarf; be warned that there will probably be pools of water underneath it, which you can mop up if you want! Now roll the whole mat as you would a rolling pin, at least one hundred times, putting as much pressure on it as you can.

Unroll the mat and straighten out the net, thus preventing any creases from forming. Then roll up again from the opposite end and repeat the rolling process another one hundred times; if you get tired doing this you could put the mat on the floor and roll it with your feet – a wonderful exercise for your thighs!

Then unroll the mat and straighten out the net again, and turn the whole thing over so that the side that has been touching the mat is now facing up. Roll up the mat and repeat the rolling for another one hundred times.

Unroll and roll up again from the opposite end and repeat the rolling for a fourth one hundred times. Now your scarf should be ready to take out of the mat.

Fold the scarf, still inside its net, into a parcel to fit in your sink. Pour hot water over the parcel, then press down on it to squeeze most of it out. Pick up the parcel and roll it between your hands for a few minutes; after this you should be able to take the scarf out of the net. Open it up, carefully at first, so that you can see if the fleece has bonded together well enough to make a strong but fine fabric. If it is still not holding together, repeat a rolling; otherwise remove the net, rinse the scarf, and dry it. You can iron it to make it smooth and flat if needed.

To make a square scarf, lay out your fleece in a large square and proceed in the same way.

APPLIED FELT

This is a completely different sort of felt, in which a woven fabric is added to the fleece. Depending upon the character of what is added, it can make a very fine felt drape and hang like a soft fine fabric, whilst at the same time adding strength to it; the fabric also introduces texture and pattern into the body of the felt itself. Like movements in art, this method seems to have been developed in different parts of the world at about the same time. For instance you may also hear the term 'nuno' felt, which is basically the same as laminated felt.

In our opinion this technique is not something to be attempted until you have made ordinary felt, as you need to know how wool reacts, and to have practised pulling out fibres in very fine amounts. Nevertheless, this is an area in which some very good feltmakers are emerging, and experimenting with new ideas. In the gallery photographs at the end of this chapter you will see the work of Janet Ledsham who incorporates real leaves into her felt; Deborah Roberts who uses fabrics to add wonderful textures to felts that could be used for home furnishings such as curtains, or for garments; Janet Mackie who uses the newest technology to add computer images to her wallhangings; and Pam Evans who adds machine embroidery to the finest felts to create wallhangings.

We therefore suggest that you make plenty of small samples of this sort of felt before you embark on a large project, as the amount of fleece you apply and the pattern you lay it on with will give a different result every time. Here we give instructions for sampling each sort of applied felt. You can then decide which sort you would prefer to use if you intend making a larger item, and it will give you an idea of how much shrinkage is involved with each technique.

SAMPLE ONE: Fleece to One Side of a Fabric

MATERIALS NEEDED

- Large mat
- Large net
- 1m (39in) of cotton muslin
- About 20g (1oz) fleece, possibly less

Open out the mat on the surface where you are to work – this should be waterproof, so use the floor if necessary. Lay out the cotton muslin on the mat, then cover it with a very fine layer of fleece so that it is thinly but evenly covered. Use different colours if you wish; but white fleece on white muslin is very beautiful when finished. Mixing in very fine fibres of silk with the fleece will add a wonderful sheen. Cover with a piece of net.

Now you will need a jug of water into which you have dissolved soap flakes or washing-up liquid. Again, the water can be hot or cold, and you may like to use gloves. Pour the water over the sample so that it is all wet. Tap the net with your hands to make sure it goes all the way through.

Roll up the mat with the fleece inside, and roll it back and fore as you would a rolling pin at least one hundred times. Then open up the mat and pull the fabric straight again. Roll up the mat from the other end, and repeat the rolling one hundred times.

Repeat this last step twice more, then remove the felt with the net covering from the mat, and fold into a neat parcel with the net to the outside of the parcel. Place this in your sink and pour hot water over it, then press down on it to remove most of the water, but leaving the parcel of felt warm.

Now lift the parcel up above shoulder level, and then throw it down onto the mat using quite a bit of force. Pick it up again, and repeat this throwing process several times.

Next, undo the parcel and refold it so that a different part of the net is on the outside, and repeat the throwing action several times. The parcel should now be starting to noticeably shrink and wrinkle.

Try to expose all parts of the net-covered fleece in turn to the site of impact. After a while you can remove the net and throw without it. This vigorous action helps the fibres to migrate through the fabric and form an entirely new sort of fabric.

When it is perfectly strong and has shrunk as much as is needed, rinse it, and finally dry it.

Take note of how much the fabric has shrunk, as you will need to know this when calculating how large to make a piece if you intend to use it for a garment.

SAMPLE TWO: Fleece to Both Sides of the Fabric

This technique is basically the same as the one described above; however, pull out a very fine layer of fleece before putting the muslin on top, then lay out more fleece on the second side. The method for felting is the same as that described above, but this will give you a smoother and stronger fabric than the first sample.

As a general guide for this method, the weight of the fabric that you use should equal the weight of fleece: so if your piece of fabric weighs 25g then you will need approximately the same weight of fleece.

For both these samples you could also use other fabrics such as silk gauze or even fine pongee, and each will give a different result; so do try and make samples of anything you intend to use later.

SAMPLE THREE: Fleece Laid to One Side of Fabric in a Pattern

MATERIALS NEEDED

As before, though very little fleece is used for this sort of felt

Spread out the mat and the fabric on the work surface; smooth the fabric out as much as possible. Start this sample by laying very fine felt all around the edges of the fabric to form a border; it doesn't matter if it overlaps the edges.

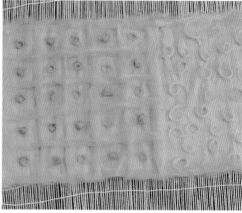

Then decide which way you are going to lay out your pattern of fleece in the middle area of the fabric. Pull out fine lines of fleece and lay them out in your chosen pattern to cover the central area of muslin.

Cover with net, and proceed as before with wetting and rolling, and also with throwing the parcel until the fabric has shrunk and the fleece has gone through to the other side of fabric.

This method gives you a sort of net with smooth areas of fleece forming the pattern, and the wrinkled and bare areas of muslin giving an added texture. The wrong side of this sort of felt is also very interesting; you will have to see which you prefer. Again, measure the finished piece, as this method shrinks enormously.

I find that these sorts of felt take much more effort than the other sorts, but they do give you a very exciting fabric when you have finished.

GALLERY PHOTOS

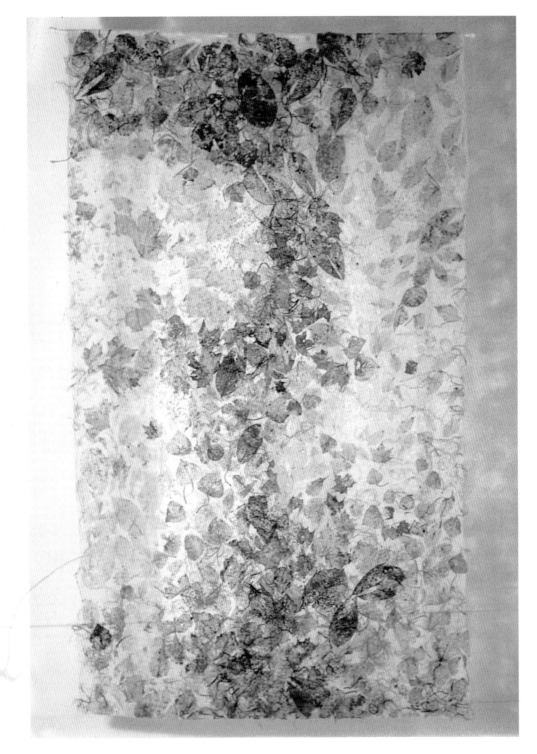

Janet Ledsham,
'Regeneration', wool and
linen felt with plant material.

Rutsuko Sakata, 'Round and Round', hats and shawl , wool and silk felt. Won prize in Japan's craft design exhibition.

Pam Evans, 'Country Dance', slashed and machine stitched.

(This page and overleaf top) Some examples of very fine felts laid on to fabric in a deliberate pattern, by Deborah Roberts.

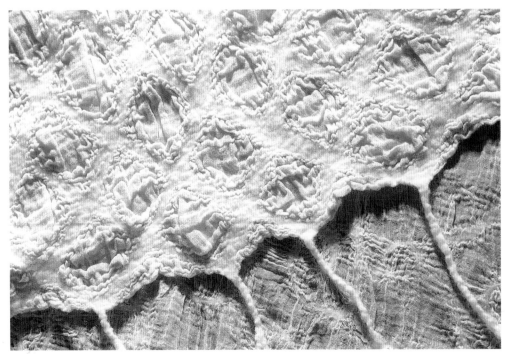

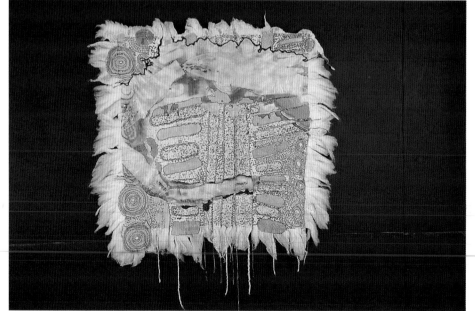

Janet Mackie, 'A Journey',
felt, digital imagery and
stitch, 1.3 x 1.3m.

6 Master Workshop Three-Dimensional Projects

The projects in this chapter use a combination of all the methods we have already discussed and used, besides adding some new elements. Thus:

For the hat we use the resist method and add the shaping part using a hat block. Trimmings are made using any method you choose.

For the fish and witch puppet we make felt over a foam base and add flat felts.

For the pots we select or fashion something solid into the shape we need, and form the felt over it; it is removed before finishing.

For the flowers we add wire to the felt so that we can alter the shapes when they are finished.

For the masks we use flat felt and stiffen it before moulding it over a form.

FLAT METHOD

Hat

MATERIALS NEEDED

- Towel
- Beachmat or blind
- Net
- Plastic resist
- Approximately 100g (4oz) fleece in the main colour
- Small amounts of fleece for decorations
- Hat block, or metal or ceramic bowl which will fit closely over the head

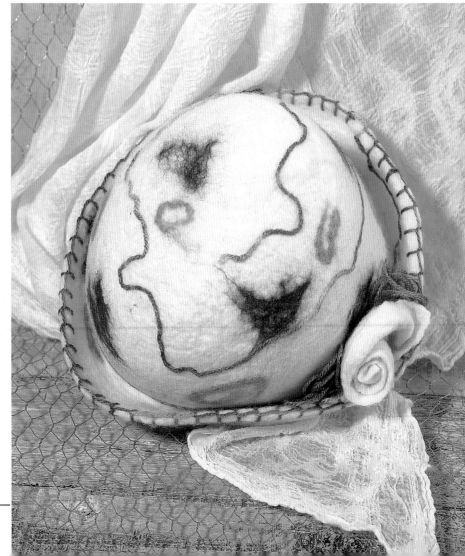

Christine Lewis, simple cloche hat.

The resist pattern for this is bell-shaped and must be half the circumference of your head plus about 5cm (2in) wide. Start as with the resist method, by putting a towel on your work surface and then laying the blind on top and the net on that. Now place your resist pattern on the net.

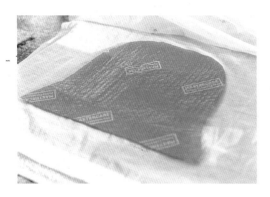

If you want a plain-coloured hat, then lay the fleece on straightaway. If, however, you want a design of some sort on your hat, start with that – you can lay it straight onto the resist pattern using fleece, or knitting yarn, or silk fibres.

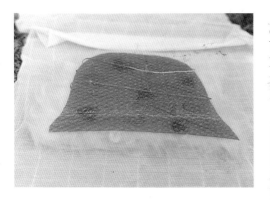

If it won't hold in place, spray the resist with some water. Note that if this is your first try at this method it is better not to have a pattern that spirals around the hat as it is quite difficult to lay out; better to wait until you have had a few attempts at this technique.

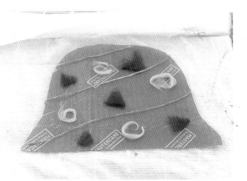

Start to layer up your main colour fleece. Leave some of the resist showing along the bottom edge.

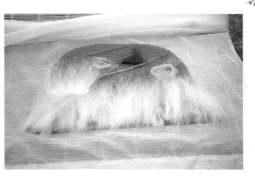

For this hat we have used five fine layers: you may decide that four is enough, but make sure there are no thin spots. Now slide one hand under the resist and place the other hand on top of the fleece layers, then flip the whole thing over.

Next, lay the pattern which you have used on the first side, directly onto the

Christine Lewis, hat with wired edges and applied wool and silk felt decorations.

resist. Fold over the edges of the lower layers which overlap the resist, making sure they lie as flat as possible and that they follow the shape of the resist closely. Spray with water if they are not holding in place.

Make the same number of layers of fleece on this side as on the other; tuck under all the overlapping ends so as to follow the shape of the resist as closely as possible.

Cover with net and felt, using whichever method you prefer. Remember to felt both sides, as the resist will prevent the water from going right through.

When the half-felt stage is reached, remove the net and turn the hat inside out so that the pattern is now showing on top; put the resist back into the centre and felt for a while longer – this will ensure that the pattern becomes firmly attached to the main body of fleece. When this stage is

reached, open up the net and remove the resist completely.

With the back of your hand inside the hat, check that no thick seams have formed where the edges of the resist were; if they have, gently stretch them out until the surface is flat again – there must be no visible seams for a hat.

Continue to felt the hood, as it now termed, until it has shrunk and hardened. At this stage it will probably appear to be too small for your head: do not worry, however, as the next process will stretch it back out again.

When you are happy that your felt is firm enough and that there are no lumpy seams, rinse and wring out most of the water.

Next we will need a hat block, if you are lucky enough to have one. These are usually made of wood and are increasingly hard to find as secondhand items. They can be bought new, but are quite expensive, and unless you intend to do a great deal of hatmaking, it is probably better to borrow one or to improvise with a bowl. If you are using a wooden block, cover it with cling film to keep the wet wool out of direct contact; then pull the hood down over the bowl or block until the top part is smooth and forming a good shape.

Hold the felt down tightly by placing a piece of strong elastic around the bottom edge of the block; this should be positioned where the edge of the hat will be turned up to form a brim. Use 2.5cm (1in) wide elastic, and cut it so that it is 2.5cm (1in) shorter than the circumference of the hat block, then stitch it together to form a circle. On traditional blocks, drawing pins could be used, but this will eventually spoil your hat block, and pins cannot be used with a bowl of any sort, so elastic is the best solution. Covered elastic is best, as rubber bands pull the fleece off with them.

Continue to pull the hood into shape through the elastic. Any areas of the hat which are not fitting tightly to the mould should be pressed with a damp cloth and a hot iron so as to shrink them into shape.

Turn up the edges, which are probably longer than you need to form the brim.

This can be trimmed as short as you wish, or cut into a scalloped or pointed edge. Leave to dry overnight. In the example shown here we have used variegated knitting yarn to blanket stitch around the edges of the brim; we have also used scraps of flat felt to make up into a flower shape to decorate one side. Equally the hat could be left plain, or some ribbon binding could be sewn around the edges.

As long as you have used enough layers of fleece the hat should be firm enough to hold its own shape easily. If it does not, the inside may be strengthened with some iron-on stiffener; it should then be lined for a neat finish, and if you wanted you could also sew a band of Petersham ribbon around the inside of the brim.

There are many ways you can ring the changes using this method for making hats, even if you use the same hat block each time; however, it is fun to look round for other things that could be used for a block mould, too. Sometimes a biscuit tin will be the right size and a more unusual shape, sometimes just changing the basic shape of the pattern to make a pointed hood or one that is wider at the top will be what you need. Experiment and see what you can come up with!

MAKING FELT OVER A FOAM CENTRE

Christine Lewis, bird, fish and dragon.

Fish project

MATERIALS NEEDED

- Foam from which to cut the shape of your proposed subject. It should not be too soft or it will lose all definition when felted; one that is used for the inside seat cushions on chairs is suitable.
- Net

- Fleece in various colours. How much you need will depend on how large a model you make; this fish finished at about 18cm (7in) long and took approximately 40g (2oz)

First decide the shape that you are going to make, and carve your foam accordingly. If you do not have a hot cutter, the best way to do the main cutting out from the block is with a breadknife, then use a pair of sharp scissors to trim to shape. Do not cut fine details, because these would be lost when the felt shrinks around the main shape; it is better to add details by another method. Don't worry too much about rough and angled edges either, as

these will also be smoothed out as the felt shrinks.

For our fish project, first of all we made the small pieces of flat felt which are to be used for the fins. There are two ways to do this: either you can make one piece of flat felt and cut two fins, or you can make two fin-shaped pieces of felt. Cut a long end on the part that will be attached to the body, then put to one side.

Start to wrap the fish-shape foam with thin layers of fleece in the colours of your choice, if possible placing each layer in the opposite direction to the one before. These lower layers will be covered up, so you don't have to worry about putting in fine detail yet.

When you have put about three layers of fleece on the foam, spray with water which has some washing-up liquid dissolved in it and rub gently with the fingers to flatten; if this proves hard to do, cover the foam shape with some net and rub through that. Do not rub for too long, however, as you will be adding more layers to this later.

Now position the fins where you want them, and secure them to the foam with a few stitches at the base where they will be covered with more fleece. Next, put down three more fine layers of fleece over the whole fish shape, remembering to go under and over the fin area so that the fins are left free to flap; the third and final layer should have any details of colour that you want to appear in the finished item. You could use fleece to make eyes at this stage, alternatively you could embroider them on afterwards, as you prefer.

Place small pieces of plastic between the fins and the body to stop them felting all the way along, then cover with net, and wet and felt as usual. The rubbing method is definitely the easiest to use at this stage. After a while, once the fleece has begun to shrink to shape and is holding together well, if you want to hurry the process along you can roll the whole thing in the mat. The foam will distort slightly, but as long as you remove it frequently and make sure it resumes the fish shape you cut, it will be fine.

Check that the fleece is felting both on top of, and under the fin area; you may

have to fold the fin back to rub under it properly. The felt will eventually harden and shrink, making the foam shape smoother.

Rinse thoroughly and leave to dry.

FELTING AROUND SOLID OBJECTS

This technique is quite fun to do with small children – for instance you can make small paperweights, or they can be embellished to make creatures; and it is also the way to make larger vessels. It is important to decide in advance whether the object you are felting over is to be removed or not, because if it is, then you must know how you are going to get it out before you begin.

Simple pebble paperweight

MATERIALS NEEDED

- Smooth pebble about the size that is easily held in the hand
- Enough fleece to cover it with about four layers

Wash the stone to remove all trace of dirt or moss, then cover it with about four layers of fleece, wrapping it round as you would wind up a ball of knitting wool.

As you become familiar with this method of modelling you will learn how much detail you can cut in the foam, and which ones are more likely to stay in place. Experiment – and have fun!

Wet the hands and soap them, or wipe them with a tiny amount of washing-up liquid. Wet the fleece-covered stone and start to rub it all over between your hands; cover it with net if this makes it easier. At first the fleece will become baggy on the stone, but as you continue to rub it will shrink and harden to fit. Finally rinse, squeezing out as much water as possible.

These can either be used as paperweights, or you could make small balls or rolls of felt and add them to make tiny creatures: what you do is only limited by your imagination.

MOULDING OVER SOLID OBJECTS

Blue head mask.

Mask

MATERIALS NEEDED

◆ Towel
◆ Mat or blind
◆ Net
◆ Fleece: how much will depend on how elaborate and how large you make your mask
◆ Face-shaped mould: this could be purpose made in plastic, or glass or wood, or you could improvise with some small-gauge chicken wire moulded into a shape
◆ PVA glue
◆ Beads and other items for decoration

We started this project by making a flat piece of felt big enough to cover the mould; however, you can take it as far out to the edges as you want. Then lay out the mat as usual and make the flat piece to hard-felt stage, then rinse and wring out as much water as you can.

Next take a small bowl and mix one part PVA glue with two parts water; you will need enough to immerse your piece of felt completely. Note that if your mould is plastic or glass you will be able to remove the mask easily when it has dried; if it is wood or plaster, however, we suggest that you cover the whole thing with cling film so that the glue does not come into contact with the mould.

Immerse the felt for the mask into the diluted PVA mixture and press well in. When it is thoroughly soaked, remove it and wring out as much of the glue mixture as possible, as too much can leave a residual layer on the felt and actually obscure its surface. Now place the felt over the mould and smooth into the folds. Leave until it is completely dry.

Meanwhile make any additional pieces of felt that you need to embellish your mask. For this gruesome example we made some small cones of resist felt which we then lightly stuffed and stitched to form horns. You could use the same principle to make an extremely large nose or some cauliflower ears: the possibilities are endless.

When your mask is dry you can remove the mould and stitch on other pieces of felt. Our example is also decorated with some dry fleece and some jewellery wire bent into decorative shapes.

This sort of mask could be used as part of a costume. The lion's head (*see* below), on the other hand, is a flat piece of felt which has been cut to shape and stuffed lightly for use as a wall hanging.

Lion's head

MATERIALS NEEDED

- Towel
- Mat or blind
- Net
- About 75g (2½oz) main colour fleece to make a 30cm (12in) head and mane
- Wool and yarn for decorating
- Embroidery threads

Make a piece of flat felt large enough to cut out your main head shape; use the scraps to cut pointed mane shapes for

decorating. The pattern for cutting the head shape is based on Chinese paper cutting, and it might be a good idea to cut it out in paper first of all, so you know

Pattern for lion's head.

how it will look, and so you end up with the size of mask you want.

Cut where the dark lines are. Join points A and B together under the nose part, and then form the nostrils into small cone shapes. All the yarn is stitched into position, and the eyes are embroidered. Make your lion as cute or ferocious as you like.

Large flower

MATERIALS NEEDED

- Soft ball about 23cm (9in) diameter
- Approximately 40g (1½oz) fleece in various colours
- Plastic-covered wire
- Net

Start by covering the ball in the colours of the inside of the flower; in our picture this was yellow. Then make about three layers with the main fleece colour – red in our example. Spray with water to hold everything in place.

Next, cut lengths of wire which will form the veins up the centre of each petal; fold over the ends so there are no sharp points that would risk breaking through the felt. Cover with another two or three layers of felt. Cover with net, then felt as usual with water and soap.

When the fabric is hard, snip into the top of the ball shape as far as the ball itself, then cut down to make petals. Remove the ball, and continue to felt inside the surface of the flower until it is hard. Rinse, and dry. With the wire inside, the petals can be bent into the shape you want. Make leaves and a stalk if you need them.

COMBINED METHODS

Witch puppet

This project combines modelling over foam with flat felt and resist felt and also miniature hatmaking.

MATERIALS NEEDED

- Foam for cutting
- Resist pattern for glove puppet
- Small resist pattern to make the witch's hat
- Towel
- Mat
- Net
- Approximately 60g (2½oz) black fleece for the cloak, puppet body and hat
- Approximately 25g (1oz) fleece the chosen colour of the face
- Scraps of white fleece for decorating the cloak

Start by making the head of the puppet as it takes a long time to dry. First, carve the foam to a rough head shape, carving only roughly the detail of a very large nose. The foam head needs to be about the size of a small melon, or twice as big as a tennis ball. Remember to allow a long neck area, because it will have the body sewn on to it.

Do not cut out the centre of the head where the fingers will go at this stage, as it would collapse in on itself when felting.

Proceed as with the fish project, and cover the foam with layers of fleece in your chosen colour. Do not cover the base where the fingers will be inserted. If you want you can spray each layer with water as it goes on, to hold it in place. We used five thin layers, each going in roughly opposite directions. Cover loosely with net, then start to felt as usual by rubbing all over. Pay particular attention that there are no bare areas forming. Again, once it has started to form the shape of the head, you can roll it in the mat to speed up the felting process – though pull it out frequently to work it back into shape. Carry on until it has hardened and shrunk. Rinse thoroughly, then squeeze out as much water as you can. Leave to dry.

Cut out the centre when almost dry.

Now, with a small pair of sharp scissors, start to remove some of the inside part of the foam where you will need to insert your fingers. This is quite tricky as the foam will have compacted, but carry on until you are happy with the space you have cut out. A pair of tweezers or small-nosed pliers will help to pull out some of the foam. Then leave to dry thoroughly. This can take a few days if the room temperature is not too warm.

Next, make the body of the puppet using a resist to make a glove puppet shape, as in the frog puppet shape. Rinse and dry. Then cut open the neck edge so that it can be attached to the head part of the puppet.

Make a flat piece of felt for the cloak. You can decorate this with moons and stars or whatever you like. Finish felting, and rinse and dry.

Lastly, make a tiny witch's hat using the resist method. Rinse and leave to dry.

When all these parts are finished and dry, they can be assembled and stitched in place. First, finish off the head part, with any stitching required; for instance, we attached two beads for the eyes – by pulling them together tightly through the foam they sink into the head. We also embellished the face with some stitching to pull the features into place and make a puckered mouth. Alternatively you could embroider a pair of eyes, or stitch on a couple that are specially made for dolls and teddy bears. If your puppet is to be used by a child, be sure to attach them firmly, or embroider them to make sure they won't come off.

For the hair, in this example we have again used some Wensleydale and mohair fleece, using long pieces stitched at a centre parting. If you do not have this you could use knitting yarn.

Lastly, sew the hat in place all around the brim, stitching into the foam. A curved needle is useful for this. Attach the neck part of the glove puppet body to the head by slip-stitching the cut edge into place through the foam. Check that your hand will fit comfortably inside the body and the foam head. Lastly, attach the cloak with some stitching around the collar area.

Your witch is ready to cast some spells.

Dragon

MATERIALS NEEDED:

- Foam for the body
- 75g (3oz) fleece
- Plastic-covered wire

First cut your body shape, which should include the head. Cut four lengths of plastic-coated wire to make the legs; these need to be about 46cm (18in) long so they can be threaded through the foam and bent into paw shapes. Then push the raw ends into the body part of the foam.

Wind small scraps of foam round the wire parts to pad them a little. As you cover the body and legs with fleece, try to apply each layer in a different direction to the previous one; spraying them with water will help to hold them flat. We used five layers for the body part, and a couple more round the legs and paws to make sure that no wire would show through when these were felted.

When you are happy with the number of layers, start to felt the whole body and

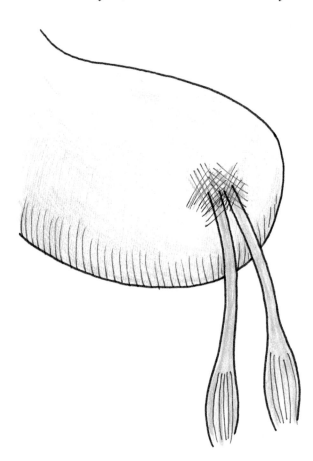

the legs; keep working until you have reached the half-felt stage.

Next, make any pieces that you want to add on to the dragon, such as the mane and tail, cover them with dry fleece, and attach them to the main body.

Carry on felting the whole animal until the felt has become firm and all the parts are completely joined together. Rinse and dry thoroughly. Finally add any embroidery features that you need.

Sculpture

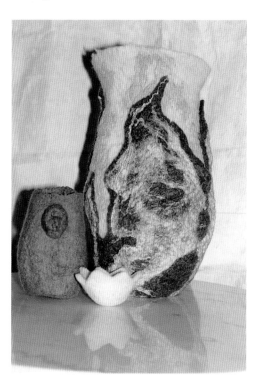

This large sculptural form is made using the resist method. It is purely decorative, so you can be as free as you wish.

MATERIALS NEEDED

- Very large wooden blind
- Large piece of bubble wrap from which to cut out the pattern
- Large net
- About 75–100g (3–4oz) each colour fleece
- Silk noils to decorate, or another colour fleece

Start by cutting your pattern from the bubble wrap; for the project described here we used a large urn shape. Then lay out your blind and the net, put your pattern on top, and put on your layers of fleece. We used silk noil for the first layer – this becomes the outside, as with the hat project; however, you can use fleece to make your design if you prefer.

To make sure this was strong and solid when complete, we used five layers of fleece to cover the pattern before turning over and repeating, just as in previous resist projects. Cover with net, then felt using your preferred method.

For this project we made two urns exactly the same size; when one was almost finished we cut into the top edge so it flopped over into petal-like shapes. We then re-felted the cut edges to make them smoother. Embroidery may be added at this stage, for extra embellishment. Press into shape whilst still damp, and allow to dry.

If your pot is not quite firm enough, try putting an old glass or metal pot inside the base of the felt to help it hold in shape.

SUMMARY

We hope that having studied thus far the techniques described in this book, you will be able to make any shape you want. There are a few other things which you could use in your feltmaking, such as adding wire to a form to make it stay in shape, but on the whole you should be able to make large pieces and stitch them together to make something sculptural, or you can make the form over a resist of some sort.

Care for your felt

Once you have completed your felt, whether it is a garment, a picture or a wall-hanging, you will want to keep it looking as good as new. Sometimes people who visit exhibitions are reluctant to buy felts and felt garments because they are worried about wear and tear and keeping them clean, but you should explain to them that this is not a problem. All woollen garments tend to 'pill' with wear, and felted garments are not immune to this. But it is possible to shave off the 'pills' without risk of making a hole, which of course would be a disaster with a knitted fabric.

Felt is naturally water- and stain-repellent, and it is even a fire-retardant material, so keeping it clean should not be too difficult. Garments can be gently washed by hand in tepid water with soap flakes or a suitable detergent. Take care not to rub the fabric as this could cause further felting or shrinkage, and rinse thoroughly to ensure that all traces of soap are removed, otherwise it will eventually rot.

Wall-hangings and rugs can be vacuumed to remove dust, though be careful to do this on a very low setting. In fact in Turkey, the final stage of preparation for new felt rugs is that they are used on the floor and swept regularly through the summer: the felt becomes shiny as a result of this treatment, and this is considered more attractive – by winter time they are deemed ready to be offered for sale!

Felt pictures can be mounted and framed in a box frame behind glass to protect them from dust and the ravages of moth and the carpet beetle.

Pests

Dogs and cats, probably your own, just love felt as a toy or bed and can do untold damage to a treasured piece. The real villains, however, are moths and carpet beetles: these are much more surreptitious in their attack, and indeed their destructive presence may not even be discovered until the eve of an important exhibition! Holes in felt are beyond redemption, so take action regularly and often with repellents to prevent these creatures getting a foothold: there are various brands of moth-repellent on the market, or you could concoct your own pot pourri using natural and environmentally friendly ingredients. These might include aromatic herbs such as tansy, lavender, feverfew, santolina and lemon verbena, dried and mixed with whole cloves, cinnamon, bay leaves and orris root. Leave this mixture to 'cure' for a couple of weeks, then pack handfuls into sachets and place with your stored felts in sealed polythene bags. This should repel moths or carpet beetles; it will not, however, have any effect on greedy larvae.

If this fails and you do find moth eggs in your felt, you may be able to kill both eggs and larvae by deep freezing them. Put the felt into a polythene bag and freeze for at least forty-eight hours; when you take it out, shake it well and the eggs should fall off.

The carpet beetle can be an even bigger problem, and once it invades your home it is extremely difficult to eradicate. It will fly into the house in summer when the windows are open, and lay its eggs in the carpets by the skirting board, in the folds of curtains, and in the creases of stored woollens. In felt the larvae burrow through the layers, eating their way out and leaving very noticeable holes. It is therefore vital to inspect stored felts regularly, and to shake them to dislodge the eggs. If you do find eggs, crush them to make sure they are dead. Do not forget to inspect framed felts as well, because these insects are minuscule and can even get behind the glass.

Clothes moth   Clothes moth larva

Carpet beetle   Carpet beetle larva

Pictures of the bugs

Know Thine Enemy...

THE CLOTHES MOTH

The insignificant clothes moth is tiny, only 5–8mm ($\frac{3}{16}$–$\frac{5}{16}$in) long; it has shiny yellow front wings, is seldom seen and it rarely flies, preferring to live in dark corners or folds of cloth where it lays its eggs. The real damage is done by the larvae, small cream caterpillars with brown heads, about 12mm ($\frac{1}{2}$in) long, which feed on wool and silk products.

THE CARPET BEETLE

The carpet beetle is black and no more than 5mm ($\frac{3}{16}$in) long, oval in shape, with a concealed head. Its larvae are about the same size, but golden brown and with a tuft of tail hairs. A 'varied' carpet beetle is a minuscule 3mm ($\frac{1}{8}$in) long; it has a round body marked with a mottled pattern of yellow, white and orange scales on a black background. Its larvae have light and dark brown stripes across the abdomen, and several tufts of tail hairs.

7 Profiles of Leading Artists

JEANETTE APPLETON

Jeanette Appleton trained in textiles at Loughborough and Goldsmiths School of Art, and recently took her Fine Arts degree at Middlesex University, London. As part of her research she travelled to Scandinavia, Australia and America. Jeanette's work expresses concepts of space and images, with reference to cultural and historical connections both in landscapes and in the city.

The emphasis is on colour-mixing and the embellishment of the felt surface, using acid dyes and hand-carding to produce layers of fused colour. Printed silk and silk fibres are embedded during the felting process. She will often use various appliqué techniques too, and also hand and machine stitchery and printed dyes. These techniques help to evoke surfaces with qualities such as ageing and transparency, often by layering different, contrasting media. Jeanette is a visiting lecturer at various colleges, and runs courses and workshops.

STEPHANIE BUNN

Stephanie Bunn studied the people of Kyrgyzstan for her anthropology PhD, concentrating in particular on their yurts, feltmaking and oral poetry. In 1991 she was invited to take part in the UNESCO Steppe Route Project, which involved travelling across Soviet Central Asia along the Silk Road from Turkmenistan in the west to the Chinese border in the east – described as a 'living lesson in Central Asian culture past and present'. There have been several more visits since, resulting in exhibitions at the Museum of Mankind, and in the publication of many articles in textile journals.

MARY BURKETT

Mary Burkett was an art teacher when she discovered felt on her travels in Syria in 1962. She saw some people rolling a bundle of something in a bed of leaves, a bundle which turned out to be felt. This intrigued Mary so much that she spent all her spare time for the next sixteen years researching felt in the East. The fruits of this labour still have wide-reaching effects, starting with an exhibition and a book called *The Art of the Feltmaker* in 1979, and continuing today with the International Feltmakers Association of which she is a founder member and president. She is known to feltmakers all over the world as the 'Mother of Felt'.

JENNY COWERN

Jenny Cowern studied painting at the Royal College of Art, and she has won many major awards. Her work is featured in many publications, and has been exhibited in group exhibitions and one-man shows in the UK and Europe.

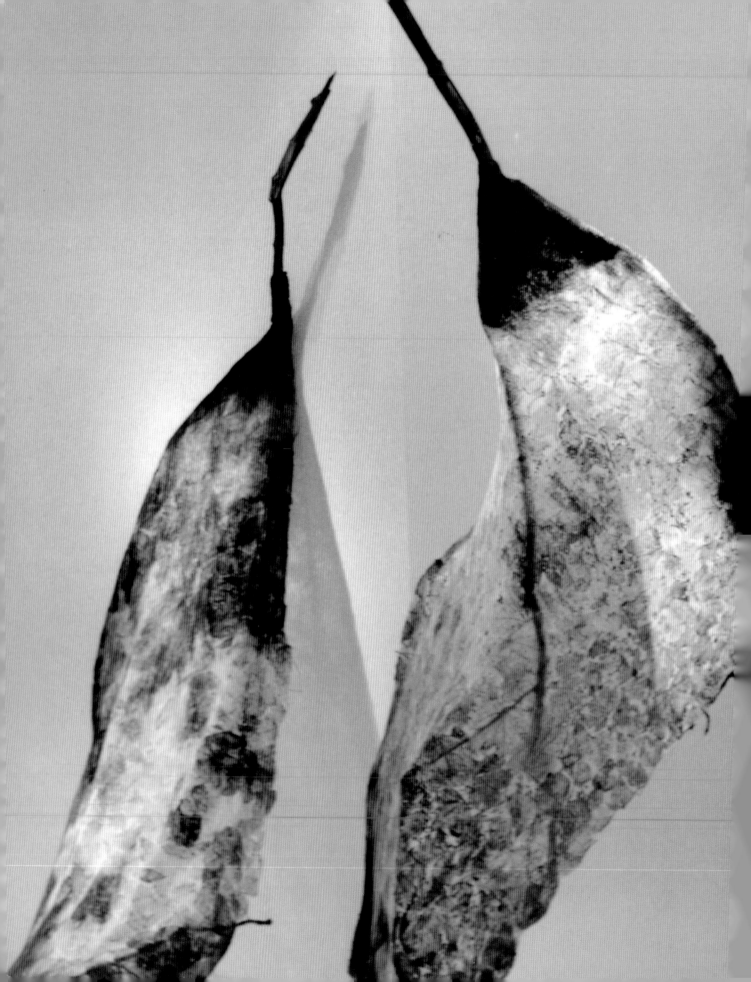

PAM EVANS

Pam Evans is a Licentiate of the Society of Designer Craftsmen. She is interested in text as a visual form, using poetry as inspiration. Her felt is made with random line and shape and she allows images to suggest themselves to her, then freely machine-stitches directly onto it, creating the spiritual quality she wants to achieve.

ROSWITHA HOWELLS

A spinner, weaver and feltmaker whose work is inspired by natural forms and poetry. She has exhibited widely in the UK.

JORI JOHNSON

An American artist now living and working in Japan, Jori Johnson is immensely influential in feltmaking today. She would like to see feltmaking more widely appreciated as a visual art, and its integration into the modern world of fashion fabrics. In her work she enhances and exaggerates the surface possibilities of felt, embedding silk organza, mohair yarns and linen into a foundation of mixed coloured wools, then overdyeing areas to produce extraordinary sections of deep colour, whilst preserving other portions of the fabric by resist dyeing. She exhibits all over the world, her work is represented in private and public collections, and she has won international awards.

JANET LEDSHAM

Janet Ledsham studied Fine Art at Manchester University. She now lectures at the School of Fine and Applied Arts at the University of Belfast, and is a member of the 62 Group of Textile Artists. She has exhibited in Europe, Japan and the United States of America, and her work is held in both public and private collections. Since moving to Ireland, Janet has taken the landscape as her inspiration, especially the moorland bogs of Counties Antrim and Donegal.

She incorporates natural materials, collected on location, into the substrata of the felt, creating a wide range of rhythms and patterns with texture and subtle colours. Free machining and hand-stitching are used as further embellishment, for quilting and attaching the materials, all of which have so far proved surprisingly robust! This format was used for 'Canopy', which was inspired by the mantle or 'kapenek' worn by shepherds in Afghanistan and Turkey.

JANET MACKIE

Janet Mackie is a Licentiate of the Society of Designer Craftsmen and exhibits widely. She takes her inspiration from digital imagery, and combines felt with other fabrics and stitchwork. The felt is loosely made, representing one of the oldest crafts, and is a vehicle to provide a constructed surface. Digital imagery represents a new, constantly advancing technology, and the stitchwork binds them together.

ALEXANDER PILIN

Although Pilin's felt is not shown in this book, he is a very influential figure in the world of feltmaking: he is known as the 'Father of Felt', and you can see his work on the internet (*see* below). His first career was as an engineer and scientist, but he had a great talent for invention and he wanted to use this talent to make unusual things. He quickly mastered many different materials, including

(Opposite) Janet Ledsham, 'Underwood', hand made felt incorporating natural plant material. The delicate felted lengths are interwoven with branches to create sculptural effects reminiscent of the woodland canopy.

leather and clay, making leather body shapes and exploring the tempo and rhythm of movement. The transition from leather to felt was a natural one for him, and he began to make woven felt lace cloaks and mantles with all the qualities of refined calligraphic abstraction, elegant lace-like felt sandals with leather soles, and very wearable hats which frame the face beautifully.

(Internet details:
http://www.udm.ru/culture/Pilin)

DEBORAH ROBERTS

Deborah Roberts is an embroiderer and feltmaker who has experimented widely with the 'Nuno' technique to produce delicate-looking but versatile fabrics for interior and fashion use. She exhibits internationally and holds workshops.

RUTSUKO SAKATA

Rutsuko Sakata, a Japanese artist, studied woven textiles in Finland and discovered felt about ten years ago when looking for a technique for a three-dimensional form which was soft and wearable. She now makes hats, scarves and clothes with merino wool and silk, and also uses silk cloths such as organza and gauze. Her award-winning designs have been exhibited internationally.

HELEN TOWELL

Helen Towell is a weaver who came to felt when engineering with wool; she likes experimenting with its immediacy. She learnt to make toys with May Hivistendal in Norway, using traditional Scandinavian techniques. Helen's humorous, perky birds are a good vehicle for having fun with colour, and are ripe for embellishment with buttons and beads and threads.

(Previous page) 'Tree relic'
(Above) 'Fantasy fungi'
both by Ros Howells.

Museums to Visit

Feltmakers seem to be great travellers, from a nomad in Mongolia to an American surfing the internet. They are teachers who are open-minded and willing to be taught. If you would like to see some of the wonderful ancient or ethnic felts we've told you about, here are the details of a few museums and galleries.

The United Kingdom
The Turkmen Gallery
8 Eccleston Street
London SW1 9LT

The Horniman Museum
100 London Road, Forest Hill
London SE23 3PQ

Whitworth Art Gallery
Manchester

France
Musée de Feutre
Place du Colombier
0821 Mouzon

Wool Museum
Voyage du Pays du Mouton et de la
    Laine
Les Bergerades,
07190 St Pierreville
Ardeche

Denmark
Nordjyllands Museum
Koing Christan Alle 50
DK-9000 Aalborg

Russia
The Hermitage
St Petersburg

Holland
Nederlands Textielmuseum
Goirkstraat 96
5846 GN
Tilsburg

Suppliers

Adelaide Walker
2 Mill Yard Workshops
Otley Mills
Ilkley Road
Otley LS21 3JP
Tel. 01942 85012/600643
*Dyed tops, merino and various breeds.
    Also silk and vegetable fibres, books.*

The Handweavers Studio
29 Haroldstone Road
London E17 7AN
Tel. 0181 521 2281
*Fleece, fibres, yarns, equipment, dyes,
    books.*

Hilltop
Dept 8, Windmill Cross
Canterbury Road
Lyminge
Folkstone
Kent CT 18 8HD
Tel. or fax 01303 862617
Email: handspin@aol.com
Fibres, books.

Wingham Wool Work
Freepost
70 Main Street
Wentworth
Rotherham
South Yorkshire S62 7NT
Tel. 01226 742926
Fax 01226 741166
Fibres and equipment.

Fibrecrafts
Style Cottage
Lower Eashing
Godalming
Surrey GU7 2QD
Tel. 01483 421853
Fax 01483 419960
Email: fibrecraft@aol.com

Fibrecrafts
Low Garth
Penruddock
Penrith
Cumbria CA11 0QU
Tel. 01768 483492
*Dyed wool tops, natural and synethic
    fibres, dyes, hand and drum carders,
    books.*

Treetop Colour Harmonies
The Mill
Tregoyd Mill
Three Cocks
Brecon
Powys LD3 0SW
Tel. or fax 01497 847421
Silk fibres and silk blends.

The Byre
Loch Doon
Dalmellington
Ayrshire KA6 7QE
Tel. or fax 01292 551021
*White and coloured merino tops, luxury
    fibres and equipment.*

(Opposite) Rutsoko Sakata,
laminated felts.

Anna Rooth
Gotland Sheepskin
Hooklands
Scaynes Hill
West Sussex RH17 7NG
Tel. or fax 01444 831325
Gotland fleeces, wool, wheels, weaving.

Hop Garden
Skenfrith
Abergavenny
Gwent NP7 8UF
Tel. 01600 84607
Fibres and books.

Moral Fibre
Anne Belgrave
Old Mill
Kinsham
Presteigne
Powys LD8 2HS
Tel. 01544 267997
Natural, undipped and undyed fleece.

Atelier Feltmaking Tools
Atelier Camelot
Hooe
Plymouth
Devon PL9 9RJ
Tel. 01725 403321
Email: feltools@ateliers.demon.co.uk
Felting needles.

InterWeb
John Smith
3 Wembdon Hill
Wembdon
Bridgewater TA6 7PX
Tel. and fax 01278 428144
Hand needlelooms.

Bibliography

Belgrave, Anne *How to Make Felt* (Search Press 1995).

Beverly, Gordon *Feltmaking, Traditions, Techniques and Contemporary Explorations* (Watson Guptill Publications 1980).

Brown, Victoria, *Feltwork* (Lorenz Books, Anness Publishing, 1996)

Bunn, Stephanie 'Feltmaking in Central Asia: The Kryghyz Yurt' *Echoes* no. 29 (International Feltmakers Association).

'Kryghyzstan Diaries' *Echoes* no. 43 (International Feltmakers Association).

'Mongolian Felt Carpets' *Echoes* no. 35 (International Feltmakers Association).

'Steph's Week' *Echoes* no. 49 (International Feltmakers Association).

Burkett, Mary E. *The Art of the Feltmaker* (Abbot Hall Gallery, Kendal, Cimbria 1979).

'The Kingdom of Loulan – Eternal Beauty' *Echoes* no. 35 (International Feltmakers Association).

'Felt on the Isle of Man' *Echoes* no. 28 (International Feltmakers Association).

'Gravestone of a Roman Archer 200–300 B.C.' *Echoes* no. 33 (International Feltmakers Association).

'Caucasian Mummies From Xinjiang' *Echoes* no. 36 (International Feltmakers Association).

Dalal, Meike 'Not that the Roof is Falling In' *Echoes* no. 47 (International Feltmakers Association).

Daniel, Peter 'Feltmaking – The Needle-Punched Method' *Echoes* no. 39 (International Feltmakers Association).

Evans, Inge *Feltmaking Techniques and Projects* (A&C Black 1987).

Freeman, Sue *Feltcraft, Handcrafted Felt from Fleece to Finished Projects* (David and Charles 1988).

Johnson, Jori 'Happy and Healthy Feltmaking' *Echoes* no. 39 (International Feltmakers Association).

'The Shoso-in "Kasen" Carpets of Nara' *Echoes* no. 35 (International Feltmakers Association).

Lang, Marlene 'Feltcraft in Turkey' *Echoes* no. 33 (International Feltmakers Association).

Martin, Peter 'The Riddle of the Sands' *Sunday Times Magazine* (31 January 1999).

Milne, Joy 'As Felt Becomes an Art Form in Britain' *Echoes* no. 54 (International Feltmakers Association).

Nagy, Mari and Vidak, Istvan *Felt Toys* (Kecskemet-Reigate 1997). (Can be obtained from The Toy Museum and Workshop, H6000, Kecskemet, Gaspav AU 11, Hungary. Tel: 00 36 76 476462.)

Randall, Leslie 'Hot Foot to Felt in Cornwall' *Echoes* no. 28 (International Feltmakers Association).

Rozenberg, Dr Natalya 'Alexander Pilin' *Echoes* no. 46 (International Feltmakers Association).

Rudenko, Sergei I. *Frozen Tombs of Siberia: The Pazyryk Burials of Iron Age Horsemen* (J.M. Dent and Sons, London, 1970).

Selse, Elisabeth 'Yurt Alert' *The World of Interiors* (March 1999).

Sjoberg, Gunilla P. *New Directions for Felt – An Ancient Craft* (Interweave Press 1996).

Smith, Shelia and Walker, Freda *Feltmaking – The Whys and Wherefores* (Dalefelt Publications, Thirsk, Yorkshire, 1995).

Spark, Pat 'Feltmaking Terminology in North America' *Echoes* no. 32 (International Feltmakers Association).
Scandinavian Style Feltmaking: A Three-Dimensional Approach to Hats, Boots, Mittens and Other Useful Objects (available from Patricia Spark, 1032 SW Washington Street, Albany; or USA 97321).

Woods, Lynn 'Beating the Moth Problem' *Echoes* no. 34 (International Feltmakers Association).

List of Web Sites

IFA – http://www.antel.demon.co.uk/ifa/ifa.htm
Mongolian felt tent – http://www.dynamicdiagrams.com/design/felt/-tent/felt-tent-fr.html
Birgitte Krag Hansen – http://www.geocities.com/paris/metro/3075/uk-home-fr.html
North America Felters List – http://www.ncn.com/~spider/spark.htm
Sarah Lawrence – http://www.sarah-lawrence.com
http://home earthlink.net/~springhollow/
http://www.threadsmagazine.com

The International Feltmakers Association

This association was founded by a group of feltmakers who met after seeing Mary Burkett's exhibition 'The Art of the Feltmaker' at the Kendal Gallery. It promotes the work of artists, craft people and designers in felt by organizing exhibitions, lectures and workshops. The founder members came from the UK, America, Australia, Norway, Finland, Holland and Denmark, but the quarterly magazine *Echoes* is published in England. It can be obtained from the editor, Lesley Blythe-Lord, at Camelot, Amacre Drive, Hooe, Plymouth PL9 9RJ.

All the artists mentioned in this book are members of the IFA. Most are willing to hold workshops or lectures, and can be contacted through *Echoes*.

Colourful and innovative hats by Japanese feltmaker Rutsuko Sakata.

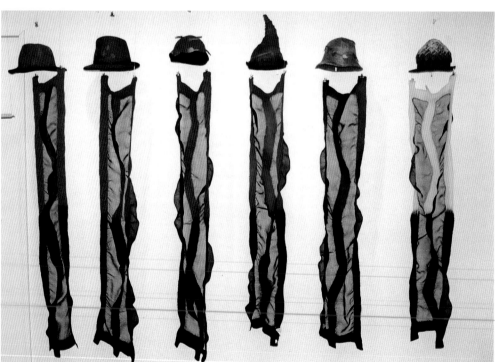

Rutsuko Sakata. Hats and Scarves – wool, silk and organza.

Glossary of Terms

ala kiyiz Pressed felt made in Central Asia. Also known as 'bright felt'.

batt The layers of carded fibres which have been prepared for felting.

carded/carding A drum or hand-held block of wood with small hooks through which the fleece is drawn to separate and align the fibres prior to layering up in a batt for felting.

chij A reed mat used by nomadic people in Central Asia on which to lay out the fleece. It is also used as a screen inside a yurt.

cobweb felt Very fine layers of fleece which remain fine and slightly transparent after felting, with a web-like appearance.

crimp The natural kinkiness or waviness along the length of the wool fibre.

felt A pressed, matted fabric formed by heat, moisture and friction, causing the wool fibres to interlock without spinning, weaving or knitting.

felting needles A single needle or a group of six needles. Used increasingly for modelling with felt. They can also be used to hold features in place, without stitching, before felting.

fleece The shorn wool of a sheep. It can mean the whole fleece or simply a mass of fibres.

fulling Also known as 'milling'. The final process of feltmaking, which comes after hardening and further compacts the felt by rubbing, rolling and pounding.

ger A felt tent used as a dwelling by nomadic peoples in Central Asia. *See also* yurt.

harden(ing) The shrinking of the soft felt to the required size, to the point where it has become a solid mass which will not come apart with gentle pressure.

half-felt When the felting process has just begun and the fibres are beginning to form a sheet of fabric, but have not yet begun to shrink. Shapes can be cut out of it for use in some feltmaking design techniques. Also known as 'pre-felt'.

inlay The name given to a technique of felt design. Shapes are cut out of half-felt and laid on top of unfelted fibres. The whole lot is then felted together and the half-felted pieces keep their original shape.

kepenek A felt mantle or hooded cloak worn by shepherds in Turkey and Afghanistan.

kurak shydak A technique of patchwork felt design used in Central Asia.

laminated felt Fleece is laid on top of a fine woven fabric such as silk. The two fabrics are felted together until the wool has shrunk, creating wonderful textures with the unshrunken woven fabric. Also known as applied felt and 'nuno' felt.

lap A layer of carded wool from hand- or drum-carding. When rolled it is also known as a 'rolag'.

merino A breed of sheep, mainly from Australia, whose fleece is excellent for feltmaking.

mosaic felt Two layers of contrasting colour felts are cut into patterns, reassembled and felted together to form a mirror image. *See also* shyrdak.

mother felt An old felt which is used in place of the *chij* or reed mat. The fibres are layered on top of the old felt, then rolled up in it and dragged across a field (or steppe) in Mongolia. The resultant new felt is called the 'daughter felt'.

needle felt Mechanically made felt, primarily for commercial and industrial use. Thousands of barbed needles are punched quickly through layers of fleece to entangle the fibres and produce a web of fabric. No water is used.

noil Short fibre combed from yarn during preparation.

pH factor The measure of acidity or alkalinity.

resist A technique to stop fleece from felting to itself. Used when making three-dimensional felt such as hats and slippers.

shydak A mosaic felting technique for rugs made in Krygyzstan and Kazakhstan.

shyryk Quilted felt made in Kyrgyzstan.

silk caps The name given to the stretched-out cocoon of silk because it is the shape of a knitted hat. It is made up of several layers which can be used individually or together.

syrmak Couched felt made in Kyrgyzstan. It can also be a particular combination of appliqué, mosaic and quilting techniques.

tops Commercially prepared fibres which have been carded and combed into long strips like loose rope. The long fibres are parallel and excellent for felt-making. Also called 'roving'.

yurt A felt tent used by the nomadic peoples of Central Asia. The word is more properly used to denote the site or space on which the tent or *ger* is put. *See also* ger.

Index